"Most people are not willing to do the hard work that it takes to make success easy."

– *Jeffrey Gitomer*

THE FIRST WRITINGS OF

NAPOLEON HILL

Truthful Living

*Truthful Living Will Guide Your Pathway to a
Happy, Healthy, Wealthy Lifestyle and Life*

Foreword, Actions, and Annotations by
JEFFREY GITOMER

Published by Amazon Publishing, Seattle
www.apub.com

Amazon, the Amazon logo, and Amazon Publishing are trademarks of Amazon.com, Inc., or its affiliates.

ISBN-13: 9781503942011
ISBN-10: 1503942015

Cover design by Faceout Studio, Jeff Miller

First Edition

First Printing October 30, 2018

Foreword, Actions, and Annotations by Jeffrey Gitomer

Edited by Jennifer Gluckow

Book Designer: Mike Wolff – mike@16bookdesign.com

Printed in the United States of America

The First Thoughts of the Father of American Achievement and Wealth

by Jeffrey Gitomer

In 1917, 20 years before the publication of his magnum opus, THINK AND GROW RICH, Napoleon Hill began his career as a teacher, philosopher, and writer at the George Washington Institute in Chicago. There he taught courses on advertising and selling, but rather than focusing on the more technical aspects of those subjects, he structured his courses around the notion that attitude, belief, hard work and personal development were the keys to achievement.

As a teacher and a writer he intuitively understood that in order to get his students to succeed, they had to start with the foundation of believing in themselves, having a positive attitude, and making a plan before they could ultimately achieve their purpose.

Mindful of the potential legacy of these teachings, and proud to have created them, Hill wrote, typed, and hand signed each lesson.

Over the next two decades, Hill would go on to hone his craft and substantiate his original thinking by interviewing and writing about the most successful people of his time: icons like Edison, Firestone, Burroughs, and Schwab. Over the course of 45 years, Hill expanded the positive principles he wrote about and spoke about in 1917; penned ten books that have sold more than 100,000,000 copies; delivered thousands of talks and lectures; and became world renowned as the leader in self-help, personal development and positive attitude. One hundred years later, he still holds that global position.

But what of those original lessons on life Napoleon Hill taught in 1917? Long the subject of rumors and speculation, they were thought lost to history – until now.

THE BOOK: TRUTHFUL LIVING

A few years ago, the Napoleon Hill Foundation uncovered Napoleon Hill's ORIGINAL writings and teachings. These are not just Hill's first writings, they represent the fundamental and foundational thinking that created his legacy.

Napoleon Hill began his career as a college professor in Cleveland delivering lectures and lessons, and had the presence of mind to document them. These lessons and lectures were penned 20 years before the immortal *Think and Grow Rich* was published. These are in fact the *first documented writings* of Napoleon Hill.

These are Hill's original thoughts and ideas about how to focus on your major goals, have a great attitude, and become successful. These are his first lectures, lessons, and writings. At the same time Hill was teaching advertising and selling, he was focusing on attitude, self-belief, writing, persuading, and philosophy of life and living.

These pages of *Truthful Living* contain Hill's original writings and lectures from 1917. *Think and Grow Rich* was published in 1937. And Hill's immortal sales book, *How to Sell Your Way Through Life*, was published in 1939. The original lessons and lectures in *Truthful Living* served as the foundation of his philosophy, strategy, and thinking for his entire body of work. Genuine classics. Genuine genius.

I have been given the honor by the Napoleon Hill Foundation to edit and annotate these writings for the 21st century. With as much integrity as I possess, I have stayed true to the concepts and meaning that Hill was trying to transfer. Here's why…

In 1971 when I was first exposed to Napoleon Hill, I was a member of a fledgling sales team and less than impressed with the prospect of learning about "positive attitude." In training with my fellow salespeople, I was literally forced by my peers to study Hill's book every day. We had a morning sales meeting where each of us was assigned one chapter in the book to "report" on. After a while I began to "get it" and during the second read of the book, only one month later, and daily group discussion with my fellow salespeople, I became both aware and enlightened that *Think and Grow Rich* was a book designed and destined to change my life.

Actually, I read *Think and Grow Rich* 10 times that year – studied and implemented both the principles and the directives. The result for me has been an unbreakable positive attitude and steadfast march toward success over the past 45 years.

I have had a decade-long affiliation with the Napoleon Hill Foundation. I create Hill's weekly newsletter, *Napoleon Hill Yesterday and Today*, and for the past ten years have grown it to more than 50,000 readers.

As a result of my positive long-term connection with the Napoleon Hill Foundation, I have been asked and authorized to compile and annotate the ORIGINAL writings (1917) of Hill in producing this book.

As eloquent as Hill was, his words were spoken and written 100 years ago. Not only has time changed, so has the language and lexicon.

With the rare endorsement of the Napoleon Hill Foundation, we are honored to present TRUTHFUL LIVING – a century-old, modern-day classic.

This book contains the first (annotated) writings of Napoleon Hill that will impact and inspire you and readers all over the world.

There are twenty-three lessons and lectures about truth, focus, integrity, desire, decisions, attitude, beliefs, goals, and living. Although written 100 years ago, all of them are timeless gems that have been lightly edited and annotated where appropriate into 21st-century words and strategies, while still maintaining the energy and importance of the work as written in 1917. These are Napoleon Hill's ORIGINAL thoughts, and FIRST delivered works.

At the end of each lesson I will give you real-world strategies that are easy to implement, and will have a huge impact on life, family, business, and earnings.

Truthfully yours,

Jeffrey Gitomer
King of Sales

"Think the thoughts, take the actions, and day-by-day success can be yours."

– Jeffrey Gitomer

"This book by itself is not life-changing, but your actions combined with the wisdom and challenges of this book will make you a more successful and wealthier person."

– Jeffrey Gitomer

Truthful Living

Table of Contents

"First comes thought; then organization of that thought into ideas and plans; then transformation of those plans into reality. The beginning, as you will observe, is in your imagination."

— *Napoleon Hill*

Lesson Number

1

Success Is Up to YOU

G **GITOMER INSIGHT:** Words change lives. *Truthful Living* is a double opportunity if you read and study this book. The first opportunity is information. You will be informed about life and success to the edge of your gray matter. There are hundreds of aha! moments inside each lesson.

The second opportunity is the challenge to do something with the information you've been provided. That's the hard part. Thousands and thousands of people will read this book, but less than 5% will adopt the principles, take the action necessary, and receive the rewards presented to you over the next 200-plus pages. If you're looking to be in the top 5%, you can find the formula on the pages that follow. The formula will seem simple, but with all things Hill, simple is never easy.

There will be no confusion in the words of Hill, even though they are 100 years old. His declarative statements and sentences…"Success is up to you" and "demand success" require no interpretation whatsoever, but they do require hard work and dedication. Dig in. Study hard. Take action for yourself. And earn what you deserve. The door of *Truthful Living* is wide open…walk in!

Ǵ GITOMER NOTE: At the turn of the 20th century, women were largely omitted from business and personal development writings. Although I think of men and women equally (I am blessed with 4 daughters and 4 granddaughters), I am trying to stay as authentic to Hill's writings as possible. Please don't let the omission of a pronoun dissuade you from reading and learning this valuable and life changing information.

As you undertake this book, remember your success will depend very largely on the following:

FIRST: The manner in which you study. You must learn to read between the lines as well as on them – that is, you must see the principle that is behind the mere words in your textbooks.

SECOND: You must go at this book just as you would if you were being paid real money to get all there is in it.

THIRD: You must be enthusiastic, persistent, and determined to WIN! You must look ahead one, two, or even five years from now and see yourself as a success, and at the same time you must fully realize that the pay you receive will depend largely upon how well you master this book.

FOURTH: You must be systematic in your studies. Set aside a certain hour each day for study and let nothing interfere with your work on your lessons during that hour. Remember that everything we do is more or less a habit, and that we can cultivate the "study" habit as easily as we can the "loafing" habit. Get into the habit of studying and soon it will come as natural as the eating of a meal.

"The ability to succeed
is a matter of
self-inspiration and a
full understanding of
human nature and a
knowledge of
your own mind's
latent powers."

– *Napoleon Hill*

FIFTH:

Believe in yourself! The reason so many fail is because they set so small a value on their ability to accomplish anything they undertake. Self-confidence is the very warp and woof of success.

G GITOMER NOTE: **Please go back and reread this formula because it contains the recipe for success in this book and in your life. It, like the rest of this book, is inspirational and challenging. Take it. Do it.**

Writing, for instance, is one of the keys to successful living. Before you can write effectively, you must believe that you can do it. SELF-INSPIRATION is closely akin to self-confidence. You get inspiration from the outside, it is true, but it must go through the electrodes of that wonderful mind of yours and take on the form of your INDIVIDUALITY. It must charge your whole heart, soul, and body as an electric battery is charged with electricity. Enthusiasm is simply a matter of SELF-INSPIRATION, nothing more nor less.

If I stopped right here, you would know but little more about how to acquire self-confidence, enthusiasm, and self-inspiration than you did before. IT would be just like telling a person to be honest if he would be successful (something which is quite obvious), but without telling him HOW TO BE HONEST.

Throughout this book we are going to deal with CAUSE as well as EFFECT. To get back to first cause in the acquirement of these desirable qualities which are here mentioned, let me give you some definite instructions to follow – AN ADAPTATION FROM MY OWN PERSONAL PHILOSOPHY WHICH I HAVE FOLLOWED FOR YEARS:

"Any idea, plan, or purpose may be placed in the mind through repetition of thought."

– Napoleon Hill

Repeat the following lines just before retiring at night and just after getting up in the morning, continuously for the next ten days:

Affirm Your Success!

1 – I am going to become a great person!

2 – I have perfect confidence in myself!

3 – I am equal to every task I undertake, and I am going to succeed. I feel that I am on my way to the greatest success I have ever known!

4 – I am alert! I am tense and ready! All my faculties are in my instant command! I now see a hundred objects about which I would write interestingly, where I never saw one before.

5 – I am successful! I am filled with energy and power! I am brave and courageous! I see tremendous opportunities ahead of me!

6 – I am going to become master of my chosen career! I will use my personal magnetism and my ability for any purpose that may be profitable and helpful to me and my fellow men!

You want to succeed or else you would not be devoting your time to this book. I need not be a mind reader to arrive at this conclusion. Then, do not look lightly upon any task, which your instructors give you to perform.

Demand Success!

Demand it with all your heart and soul and with the utmost confidence! If you faithfully carry out the suggestions and ideas in this book, your demand will be speedily and splendidly realized.

Above all things, remember that all the work of this book, the thoughts of realization, the MENTAL DEMAND for success, must precede – not follow – practical outward effort. In more simple words, BELIEVE IN WHAT YOU ARE DOING AND IN THOSE WHO ARE HELPING YOU DO IT AND YOU ARE BOUND TO WIN! You must paint a picture of the person you want to be, and if you paint that picture on the sensitive plates of the mind vividly enough, you are sure to be just like it. You will not be disappointed. If you become a great person, it will be because you have first WILLED TO BECOME GREAT! If you fail to become a great person, it will be because your will power was of the half-hearted brand.

Make your affirmations prophetic, not mere dull statements of fact! Make your energies initiative! Hold fast to this sequence: first, demand and by demanding beget CREATIVE THOUGHT; by creative thinking, efficient work; and by efficient work, WIN!

Read these suggestions again and again! Meditate upon them! Do not look for flaws – look for thoughts – thoughts out of which to build SELF-CONFIDENCE, ENTHUSIASM, and SELF-INSPIRATION! Soon their truth and practicability will dawn upon you, and you will come into the FAITH that moves mountains of DOUBT, FEAR, and LACK OF COURAGE.

Do not attempt to expound these principles to others who have not had opportunity to see the work which is being done in this book, as you have seen it. You are preparing yourself to be a great person, a great analyst of human nature. You want knowledge that you can use commercially for the betterment of yourself and your fellow men.

"Believe in what you are doing and in those who are helping you do it and you are bound to win!"

– *Napoleon Hill*

REMEMBER, THEN, THAT ALL FORCES WHICH MAKE
FOR YOUR SUCCESS ARE WITHIN YOU! Also remember
THAT YOU WILL GET OUT OF THIS BOOK IN EXACT
PROPORTION WHAT YOU PUT INTO IT IN TIME AND
EFFORT. You CAN and MUST do for yourself.

Education is something which you must get yourself. You have
to work to get it and you have to work to keep it after you get it!
Education is a self-development process. Webster says that education
is "instruction." Personally, I do not agree with Webster. Mere
instruction is not enough. I may instruct you until I become old and
gray-headed, but if you do not actually DO SOME THINKING,
YOU WILL NEVER LEARN TO BE STRONG, FORCEFUL,
AND SUCCESSFUL.

The best teacher on our staff, from YOUR VIEWPOINT, is YOU!
By the side of this teacher every man on our staff pales into oblivion.
You will take away from this book just exactly in proportion what you
make up your mind to take – no more and no less! The best teachers
in the world could not change this.

Be courageous! Have faith in yourself! Believe you can accomplish
whatever you wish to accomplish! Encourage this self-faith and do
not let it get away from you! Believe in those who are helping you
with this book! If the negative quality of DOUBT creeps into your
mind, shake it off. Entertain no doubts as to your own ability to
master this book, or as to the ability of your instructors to help you
master it! Go at your lessons in a spirit of cheerfulness!

THEN, SEE HOW MUCH YOU CAN ABSORB FROM EACH
LESSON AND CONVERT INTO PRACTICAL USE IN
CONNECTION WITH YOUR WORK.

Jot down the thoughts which come
to you from everything you read.
Take these thoughts and build stories
around them – "human interest"
stories that will serve as attention-
getters. There is practical value
in all of this.

Do not feel that I expect you to be perfect in your work. None of us
are. The age of infallibility has not yet arrived. We all make mistakes.
That's why they place rubbers [erasers] on the ends of lead pencils.
BUT – remember that you will be nearer perfection at the end of this
book than you are now.

It is just as well to mention here the fact that your first twenty lessons
will deal largely with principles. Just as you first learned the principles of
grammar and arithmetic, and then proceeded to apply those principles,
so will you first master the principles of psychology, and then apply these
principles, as you go along in this book.

Do not become frightened at the word "psychology"! I am well
aware of the fact that for many years most people have looked upon
psychology as being a subject which only long-haired professors could
unearth. The truth of the matter is that psychology, as it should be
taught, is the most interesting and the most vital subject underlying
the great mass of commercial activity today.

What is psychology?

Look up the word in your dictionary, but before you do this allow me
to give you my conception of it. Psychology is nothing more nor less
than a thorough understanding of the manner in which the human
mind works. To understand psychology is to understand humanity. To
make practical application of psychology is to direct and control the
human mind at will – particularly your own mind!

The principles through which psychology may be used are
comparatively simple. You saw a splendid example of the practical
application of psychology in Mark Antony's speech to the Roman
mob. In that speech, through the words which Shakespeare placed
in the mouth of Mark Antony, SUGGESTION was a leading
factor which swayed the mob and caused it to do his bidding. Bear
in mind that suggestion is one of the mental phenomena known
as psychology. Suggestion is the chief factor through which the
hypnotist works. The other factor, which dove tails with suggestion,
is CONCENTRATION. All through this book you will find very
simple yet understandable and practical applications of the principles
of both SUGGESTION and CONCENTRATION.

I also believe it's just as well to inform you right now that the book
which you are beginning embodies much more than the mastery of
living. By "mastery" I mean the study of life. Before I come to details,
you must master the more fundamental PRINCIPLES through which
these details are organized and make use of.

> **G** **GITOMER NOTE: Napoleon Hill always presented**
> **the validity of challenging the big picture, then**
> **broke down the details into principles and actions.**

Among the other qualities which I intend to develop for you, through
this book, are some of the most vital essentials for success and
happiness, such as self-confidence, courage, faith, humility, a good
working knowledge of "self," etc. **No person can go through this
book without developing a much more positive, pleasing, and
forceful personality than he possessed when he began**. I give you

this information in the very beginning so you may cooperate with me more effectively because you will understand the end for which I am helping you strive.

Let me explain also, that neither "religion" nor "politics" can enter into the work that I am doing in this book. My teachings are based strictly on facts that have been tried and proved to be practical by the leading philosophers and scientists of the world. I make this explanation so you may not make the mistake of feeling that I have allowed either of these subjects to creep in where they should have been excluded, if at any time it should appear to you that some of the principles with which I deal in this book are closely related to similar principles which are being disseminated under one creed or another, in the disguise of "religion."

> **G GITOMER NOTE: Hill understood that he was teaching some of the things that religions usually dealt with, but adequately deflected the criticism and boldly declared his work secular.**

Also note well that the person who fails to realize that his success in his field of endeavor will depend, to a large extent, upon how well he acquires this viewpoint concerning "truthful living" might as well stop right here and discontinue this book. "Cleverness" and the ability to "put it over on the public" will lead any person who engages in these tactics to sure and swift defeat.

Your salary or revenue from the sale of your products or services in your field of endeavor will come from someone else. This is a fact well worth remembering, and the moment you begin to play your employer (the consuming public) false, that moment begins your downfall.

If there is one big idea that I shall constantly endeavor to develop in this book, it is the idea of building all living upon the foundation of TRUTH! Without this firm foundation, no person or business can hope to permanently succeed in this day of progressive policies.

Not only is the time coming, but it is actually here, when to tell a lie on paper, directly or by innuendo, will bring the same punishment and rebuke to the person who tells it as the same lie would bring if told orally. It is personal and business suicide to "fool the buying public."

Take the great business built by Marshall Field, John Wanamaker, Sears, Roebuck & Company, Montgomery Ward & Company, Butler Brothers, and other reliable Mail Order Houses: underlying their success you will find a fundamental principle which is responsible for that success. That principle is "TRUTHFUL ADVERTISING." These firms have always practiced the habit of sending their customers away satisfied. That is what all successful firms must do.

BUT, if you are not in the mail order business, and you are not selling advertising, this principle is equally applicable to you. More so, it is a concept bigger than business, bigger than mail order, and bigger than advertising. It applies equally to life. The key concept to understand and internalize here is just that: **TRUTHFUL LIVING**.

CAUTION: Do not read ahead in this book until you finish the lesson at hand. The average person will find it necessary to read the text at least three times before beginning to live the philosophy: the first time to get a general outline of the subjects covered, the second time for the purpose of cross-indexing the questions and the places where the answers may be found, and the third to get a final summary.

Some of the ideas are intended to test your ability to think in your own terms, and the answers will not be found in this book. When you come across an idea of this sort, use your own judgment and use it accordingly.

Before undertaking this book, I want you to fully appreciate the following:

YOU WILL GET OUT OF THIS BOOK EXACTLY IN PROPORTION TO WHAT YOU PUT INTO IT IN TIME AND EARNEST EFFORT.

A Warm Handshake by Proxy

A written visit from Napoleon Hill

Friend, reader, and student of success, we are starting on what I believe will prove to be a very pleasant and profitable journey into living your BEST life.

We will get along better on this journey if we understand each other thoroughly before we start!

Frankness is one of the virtues I possess – the one of which I am proudest. I believe in laying all of the cards on the table, FACE UPWARD, in the beginning of the game.

Now if you were here at my desk we could accomplish more in half an hour, in getting acquainted with each other, than we could through exchanging a dozen or two letters. It is exceedingly difficult to place one's thoughts on paper in such a manner that they are thoroughly and correctly understood by those who read them.

In view of this, I ask you to overlook what I believe to be your shortcomings, and I will do the same with you. If I make a mistake – as all people do at times – I ask your indulgence.

I have set aside pages for my "visits" with you after each lesson. I call them my "sacred garden spot."

I shall do my best to bring to you, through each of these "visits," some new thought, and fill you with renewed enthusiasm, hope, faith, cheerfulness, charity, and self-confidence. I shall do my utmost to help you build up the idealistic side of yourself. There will be no complaining done through these pages. They must bring only optimism and pleasant thoughts.

"If you become a great person, it will be because you have first WILLED TO BECOME GREAT! If you fail to become a great person, it will be because your will power was of the half-hearted brand."

– *Napoleon Hill*

Among our readers we have nearly all nationalities – people who belong to various and sundry religious and political organizations. It makes no difference what is your religion or politics – I am your friend! And now I shall leave nothing undone that I can do on your behalf.

Here is a thought which I want you to get well established in your mind: I cannot teach you anything unless you have implicit faith in my ability and my sincerity. Through mutual faith we can turn mountains over, so to speak, but without this we cannot work in harmony. We must be attuned to and in harmony with each other in our work as we go along. This can best be brought about by being frank with each other.

If any condition arises in your life, as you go along with your book, concerning which you wish to consult with me, feel free to come, just as you would to any other close friend. Let us understand each other all through this journey! Let us be in full harmony at every step along the way!

I am going to make of you a person who FINISHES EVERYTHING HE STARTS! This book is going to be much more than a mere book on the technique of living. You will see, long before you reach the twenty-third lesson, that the book is a builder of STRONG, MAGNETIC, and FORCEFUL PERSONALITY.

What, may I ask, is the value of a book that will do this?

You now have some negative qualities, which stand between you and the success which you are going to attain. You may know what these negatives are, or you may not know. Be this as it may, you are going to have fewer negative qualities before you finish this book. You are going to have a much more pleasing personality. You are going to possess the ability to get people to do what you want them to do because they wish to do it!

Life, ah! What a wonderful study it is!

And, what is the study of life?

Friend, I will tell you what LIVING is –

IT'S THE STUDY OF THE HUMAN MIND – OF HUMANITY ITSELF!

What, may I ask, is more interesting than this wonderful machine, which we call the human mind? What is more to be desired than the ability to control, direct, and dominate the human mind – especially our own mind?

A successful person is one who can dominate and direct his own mind and the minds of others. A wonderful power, this! Then let us use it only for legitimate and honorable purposes.

Before you finish this book you will learn a great many things about living that you probably never thought of as being connected with this subject. You will learn things about the human mind – especially your own – that you probably never thought about before.

You will learn how to select words that will play upon the emotions as an expert violinist plays upon his instrument. You will learn how to affect your friends, family, and consumers as the violinist affects his listeners when he draws the bow across the strings of his violin in harmony with the vibrations which reach your mind through your ears.

What a wonderful accomplishment this is!

You will learn that you can reach the minds of others only through the five senses of – SIGHT, SMELL, HEARING, FEELING, and TASTING. And by reaching others through those senses you will create THINKING and ACTING in your favor.

You will learn to select words, which will most effectively appeal through one or more of those five senses.

That Habit of Completing

Make up your mind right in the beginning that you are going to have to sacrifice something in order to complete this book. Everything that is worth having costs a price. The book which you have begun, while it is well sprinkled with variety and human interest, is no mere "pink tea" party.

However, there is nothing in the book which ought not to be there. Many of you have been through the mill of hard experience, and have eliminated everything that is not essential. This book does the same. Bear this in mind when you come across some problem which you believe involves more work than you would like to do – DO IT GLADLY.

As I said in the beginning, you must have faith in yourself. You must believe in me, doing exactly as I say and holding me responsible only for results in the end.

I accept responsibility for your success, only on condition that you follow my instructions, just as an obedient soldier must follow the instructions of his superior officer.

There is no red-tape between you and me. There are no formalities or invisible barriers. The latchstring is always on the outside to you. I am your teacher and friend, loyal, faithful and sympathetic, ready and willing to share your heartaches as well as your joys.

These words are not written just to fill up space! When you know me as I really am, you will be thoroughly convinced of this fact. My heart and soul are in this book which you have begun. I am interested in you and your affairs. Your friends are my friends. Your joys are my joys and your sorrows are my sorrows.

I shall strive hard always to be a bubbling spring from which you can draw new inspiration, hopes, encouragement, and self-confidence; we all need this source of inspiration. The spring is right here, waiting for you. Drink from it freely, as often as you may be thirsty, and in the years to come if I have reason to feel that through my efforts you have become a bigger, better, and more prosperous citizen of America, I shall feel well repaid for my sincere efforts to benefit you.

With every good wish for your success and happiness believe me.

Cordially, your friend,

Napoleon Hill

GITOMER'S THOUGHTFUL ACTIONS

HOW TO IMPLEMENT THIS LESSON

This first lesson should be immediately reread so that you understand both the opportunity and the challenges that face you in this book and in your life. The reason I recommend rereading is for both clarity and intention. You can intend to "read the book," or you can intend to make the book part of the fabric of your life. I recommend the latter. The second reading will clarify your intentions.

Twenty years from Hill's first writings which appear here, he will begin *Think and Grow Rich* with the phrase, "Thoughts are things." Please think of this book as the precursor and the preamble to the next step in your journey for success and wealth.

Persuasion is critical to winning in the real world. Your real world. Hill states first you must gain attention or persuasion is not possible. Seems obvious, but wait until you see the depth of Hill's words...

"It seems to me that one of the great purposes of life is to: BE HAPPY ALL THE TIME AND TO MAKE OTHERS HAPPY!"

– Napoleon Hill

Lesson Number

FINISH WHAT YOU START

 **GITOMER INSIGHT:** Are you ready to start? Are you willing to finish? It's easy to see what other people have not completed. It's much more difficult when you're looking at your own life. When you see other people, you justify it with reasons. When you see yourself, you short-circuit it with excuses and blame. Finishing what you start requires that you take cynicism and negativity and convert them into optimism and positivity. Drive. Determination. And the vision to see the outcome and take daily steps toward that goal, or as Hill would say, that "definite major aim."

One of the really worthwhile qualities which we have planned to develop in you through this course is that of FINISHING ALL THAT YOU START!

Maybe you already possess this sterling quality.

If so, congratulations! You have the first essential for success in everything you undertake. After reaching the tenth lesson, one of our students wrote:

> *"I want to say to you right here and now that I have received a thousand percent on my investment in your course, because you have made me WANT TO FINISH THINGS THAT I BEGIN! You have been so kind and patient, yet so firm and persistent with me that I have wrested from this course already the real secret to success.*
>
> *Enclosed you will find my check for the remainder of my tuition in full. I am paying this in advance on the theory that when I have paid you I will let nothing stand between me and the last lesson in this great course. The tenth lesson alone is worth ten times what you charge for the entire course. It may please you to hear that through the application of the principles laid down in the 'after-the-lesson visit' with lesson ten I have changes in my business that will net me over $1,000 a year in additional profits."*

I have quoted this letter because it is typical of others we receive from men and women all over the world who have "found" themselves through the application of the philosophy that is the very warp and woof of the course you have commenced.

Every principle laid down throughout this course has been thoroughly tried out and tested in our resident classroom here in Chicago. Our class has served as part of a human laboratory in which we have thoroughly tested every principle that we are passing on to you. Furthermore, these principles have been poured from the crucible of actual business experience of the men who built this course, covering a period from ten to thirty years.

To prove the accuracy of these principles has cost not only millions of dollars in sales and advertising campaigns, but endless and untiring effort upon part of the various members of our staff.

It is my aim to present this philosophy in as simple a manner as possible. It is also my aim to make these lessons absorbing, to fill them with life so they will breathe the very essence of the good cheer, courage, self-confidence, and optimism which we have tried to inject into them. There is a scientific reason for this, as you will learn before you reach the middle of the course.

If for any reason whatsoever, either consciously or unconsciously, you have allowed a shell of cynicism to grow around you, we intend to break this shell and remove it. No person can go through this course and be unhappy at the same time.

It seems to me that one of the great purposes of life is to:

BE HAPPY ALL THE TIME AND TO MAKE OTHERS HAPPY!

This course has been built with the object of teaching all who master it the art of true happiness.

This is not mere idealism – it is common sense as well!

"What would it profit you to become the most able person in the world if you were not happy? What would it profit you to gain anything in this world if you did not also find true happiness in your work?"

— *Napoleon Hill*

If you go about the preparation of these lessons with implicit faith in your own ability to master them and with a full understanding that you are going to get out of this course all of the practical philosophy that any person needs with which to succeed, you will have absolutely no difficulty in seeing the immediate and satisfactory results!

Confidence in yourself and confidence in us must precede everything else if you expect to make this course profitable. Neither religion nor politics has entered into this course in any manner.

This is purely a business and life course, intended to prepare men and women for successful, happy careers. We make these explanations at this time for the reason that our method of presenting this course is decidedly in advance of anything ever undertaken in the educational field.

We congratulate you upon your eligibility for admission as a student-member of this course, but WE SHALL CONGRATULATE YOU MORE HEARTILY IF YOU STICK BY THIS COURSE TO THE END AND THEREBY PROVE THAT YOU HAVE THE GOOD JUDGMENT TO RECOGNIZE REAL OPPORTUNITY FOR SELF-IMPROVEMENT, AS WELL AS DETERMINATION TO FINISH ALL THAT YOU START!

You will see that I have supplied you with questions. In answering all such questions, use YOUR OWN JUDGMENT and answer in YOUR OWN WORDS. We do not aim to make you a "Polly Parrot" student. We want to make you a thinker and a constructive planner of Sales Ideas and Life Ideas!

"First comes thought; then organization of that thought into ideas and plans; then transformation of those plans into reality. The beginning, as you will observe, is in your imagination."

– Napoleon Hill

Finish Everything You Begin

(an after-the-lesson visit with Mr. Hill)

During the past fifteen years I have had the opportunity to study at close range several of America's captains of industry. The quality in all of them that impressed me most was that of their persistence in the pursuit of one object!

- **Carnegie has concentrated all of his energies on the Steel business and has succeeded in the business.**

- **Vanderlip has concentrated all of his energies on Banking and Finance and he has succeeded in that business.**

- **Rockefeller has concentrated all of his energies on the oil business and he has succeeded in that business.**

- **Harriman and Hill stuck consistently to the Railroad business and succeeded in that business.**

- **Ford has clung consistently to the automobile business, concentrating all of his efforts on that business and he has made a success of it.**

- **Wanamaker has concentrated on his retail Department Store and made a big success of it.**

And so the story might go on and on ad infinitum. The men I have mentioned are not the only ones who have succeeded because they first decided what they wanted to do and then went ahead and did it – they are just a few of the more prominent ones!

The great value of finishing everything we start is more apparent to me because it was quite noticeable that the majority of the 10,000 people whom I have analyzed were not succeeding because they had too many irons in the fire. They knew how to do too many things and had not enough knowledge of any one particular thing.

The following editorial, which appeared in *Every Week*, shows that I am not alone in my recommendations to finish everything you start if you wish to succeed:

HEZEKIAH IS DEAD; BUT HIS FORMULA STILL HOLDS GOOD: ONE THING AT A TIME.

There is a certain man among my acquaintances who, with a little less ability, would have made a splendid success. That sounds strange, but employers of man will understand: they will have a picture right away of the kind of man he is.

In his boyhood he mowed lawns, like the other boys; also he ran a lemonade stand besides, and managed a newspaper route, and was forever figuring out a new scheme.

He graduated from high school and entered business with great promise. But he had not been at work three months before he was running a couple of little private businesses on the side.

So he has continued through life – cursed with the unhappy gift of being able to do three or four things at once. He ekes out a very fair income today, drawing it in little bits from half a dozen different sources.

But he is getting along in life, and there is no one single business of which he can say: "I made it." He has scattered himself so widely that there is not one spot in the world's life that bears the permanent imprint of his effort.

Twice he was almost broken down from overworking. And four of the men who were his boyhood playmates – men who were satisfied to mow lawns and attempt nothing else – have plugged along, each in single business, and, with far less ability than he, have reached a higher place in the world.

I was reminded of him last night, in running across a reference to Lord Mount Stephen, in the new biography of James J. Hill.

George Stephen – he became Lord Mount Stephen afterward – was the son of a carpenter in Duffton, Scotland. He worked for a time in a shop in Aberdeen, but was brought to America at an early age, and became one of the makers of Canada, and a power in the British Empire.

In 1901, visiting Scotland, he was presented with the freedom of the city of Aberdeen; and this is what he said: "Any success I may have had in life is due in a great measure to the somewhat Spartan training I receive during my Aberdeen apprenticeship, on which I entered as a boy of fifteen. To that training, coupled with the fact that I seem to have been born utterly without the faculty of doing more than one thing at a time, is due that I am here before you today. I had but few wants and no distractions to draw me away from the work I had in hand. It was impressed upon me from my earliest years, by one of the best mothers that ever lived, that I must aim at being a thorough master of the work by which I got my living; and to be that I must concentrate my whole energies on my work, whatever that might be, to the exclusion of every other thing."

Concentration – with the exception of honesty – it covers a larger measure of the secret success than any other word. I once asked a very successful man how he was able to get so much done and still have leisure time. "I pick up only one paper from my desk at a time," he said, "and I make it a point not to lay that paper down until I have settled the business that it involves."

I was present in his office when a friend came to offer him a participation in an enterprise that promised to be very profitable. He answered, "I can't do it, Jim. I don't need the money, and no amount of money could possibly compensate me for the nuisance and inefficiency of having to carry two things on my mind at the same time."

"One thing at a time" was the formula of Hezekiah, who refused to dally with sidelines or attempt more than one thing at a time. And in every work that he began, he did with all his heart – and prospered.

As I write, there is an opening in my organization that will pay the person qualified to it all the way from $5,000 to $10,000 a year.

> **G GITOMER NOTE: This would be equivalent to $70,000 to $140,000 in 2018 dollars!**

Chicago is a city of over two and a half million people, over one-fiftieth of the entire population of America, yet in all this city I know of no one having the courage to tackle this job with any reasonable assurance of filling it satisfactorily. Yet the specifications do not seem unreasonable. They only call for just the type of person that all other business houses are looking for.

What do you think of the specifications:

(1) I want a man or woman who will finish everything he or she starts, whether it is sharpening a pencil, writing a letter, or something of greater importance!

(2) I want someone who will do at least everything he is told to do, and who will not offer excuses to take the place of results.

(3) I want someone who will reach out and demand great responsibilities, taking care all the while to keep growing and getting ready to assume additional duties.

(4) I want someone who will love the job so well that he will forget hours – forget pay – forget Saturday night – forget all his own selfish interests and devote his entire time and thought to the task of carving a future out of the opportunity at hand.

(5) I want someone who will be frank and sincere with himself and all with whom he comes in contact, and who will be a living example of our slogan, "Truthful Living."

(6) I want a person who will not wait for me or some of the other officials to tell him what to do, but who will learn to see what ought to be done and do it.

(7) I want a person who is big enough to overlook the little insults which thoughtless people throw out, often unintentionally – a person who can see something good in every human being on earth – a person who will honestly strive to develop the good there is in every person with whom he comes in contact.

(8) I want a person who will believe heart and soul in everything he does in connection with his position, a person who will not misrepresent the Institute, either by direct statement or by innuendo.

(9) I want a person who will meet the public with a smile on his face – a smile that comes from the heart. I want him to shake hands with people as though he enjoyed it.

(10) I want a person who will not be jealous of his fellow-employees or afraid that one of them will get his job – a person who will help those around him to be more efficient – a person who will be happy and enthusiastic.

(11) I want a person who truly loves to serve his fellow men, and who will look upon his opportunity to do so as a welcome privilege.

(12) I want a person who is observant – who sees all that goes on around him – who can distinguish between the important and the unimportant experiences of his daily routine, retaining and classifying the former and brushing aside the latter.

(13) I want a person who knows or will take the time to learn how to eat properly – a person who will not incapacitate himself and become a "grouch" by overeating, as seventy-five percent of the people of today are doing.

(14) I want a person who will refuse to allow himself to be aroused to anger by some ill-bred person who hasn't learned the art of self-control.

(15) I want a person who believes that he ought to be paid in exact ratio to what he produces for the business, whether it is $1,000 or $100,000 a year, and who will be satisfied with that.

Those are the specifications. If you can fill them, you can have the position. Or, if it should be filled when you apply, don't worry, because I have a dozen or more friends among the Chicago businessmen who will consider that I have done them an everlasting favor by sending you to them.

Notice, in particular what I stated as the first requirement! I stated it first because it is the most important.

Now here is a very startling statement. The George Washington Institute is going to prepare you to fill this position, or one as good or better. Do not misunderstand me to say that it is going to do this without an IF, and it is this –

IF – you will follow instructions faithfully until you have turned in all of the lesson assignments and passed the final examination.

In lesson number ten we have a surprise for you. In that lesson we will tell you exactly how to prepare for this position. This lesson will bring you a message that you'll never forget as long as you live. It isn't a preachment, but a scientific, tried-and-true principle which will place you head and shoulders above that great mass of humanity that is just plodding along, barely existing.

Do not ask any questions about this lesson until you get to it for this will avail you nothing. The only way you can unlock the door to the secret of this lesson is to work for it by mastering the intervening seven lessons.

The great value of this course, as you will see as you proceed with it, is that it requires you to LEARN BY DOING! On the other hand you will be constantly aware of the fact that each lesson will bring you something that you will enjoy doing – something decidedly worth doing!

And, in closing, I might as well again state that the course you are studying is much more than a course in the technique and mechanics of learning! It is all of that, of course, but that is the least that it is.

The chief object behind this course and the George Washington Institute is to help men and women to be prosperous and HAPPY! To be happy and prosperous you must cultivate self-confidence, enthusiasm, love for humanity, and the ability to stick to everything you start until you finish it!

In lesson five we will give you your first lesson in the development of these qualities, particularly self-confidence.

Long before you reach the middle of this course you are going to see a remarkable change in your mental attitude, and you are going to be mighty glad that you joined us.

If you have been in the habit of starting things that you didn't finish, you can get back on the right track and overcome this curse of mankind by making a good job of finishing this course.

In doing this, you will have accomplished something that will be worthy to you for all the time and money you will put into the course.

Yours for finishing all that you start,

Napoleon Hill

Napoleon Hill

80 E. Randolph St.
Chicago, Ill.

GITOMER'S THOUGHTFUL ACTIONS

HOW TO IMPLEMENT THIS LESSON

Well, at least you finished this lesson. And I think you're beginning to get the idea that each lesson represents its own opportunity and certainly its own challenge for you to take new, better, and more successful actions. Keep in mind that no single lesson in this book will provide "THE ANSWER," but combined, they provide the success answers that everyone is seeking, including you. The question is: Are you willing to START and FINISH? This is a book that requires little or no investment in anything other than yourself. There's nothing to buy, there's no inventory to keep, other than the investment that you make in yourself and the inventory of the success ideas and actions that are in your brain. The time has come for you to succeed, but you cannot do it without finishing what you start.

"To be happy and prosperous you must cultivate self-confidence, enthusiasm, love for humanity, and the ability to stick to everything you start until you finish it!"

– Napoleon Hill

"The time has come for you to succeed, but you cannot do it without finishing what you start."

– *Jeffrey Gitomer*

"Thought is the beginning of all the wealth and all the mechanical or physical things created by man!"

– Napoleon Hill

Lesson Number

HOW TO THINK

 **GITOMER INSIGHT:** Hill tackles a near-impossible task challenging you to think about the way you think. What are the elements that go into your thought development process? How do you think productively? This is an insightful, fundamental lesson on the reality of thought and thinking. It reveals strategies and capabilities you may already possess, but never have uncovered or exposed.

It is altogether befitting that we discuss this subject at this time because this will start you on this course with a powerful advantage – one that will not only ensure your getting more out of the course – but which will help you also to get more out of life from this time on.

THE CAUSE OF LIFE'S MISERIES

Ninety percent of life's miseries and failures are caused by our lack of understanding of the comparatively simple principles through which we think accurately. The chief reason that ninety-five percent of the people are working for the other five percent is that ninety-five percent do not know how to think.

The reason the wealth of the world is so unevenly distributed is that the masses do not know how to think while the classes do know how!

The principles underlying accurate thought are as definable and as well understood by scientific men as are the principles of mathematics.

THOUGHT DEFINED

Before we proceed further let us define thought, not necessarily as the dictionaries do, but after our own simple fashion.

In the first place, thought is the beginning of all the wealth and all the mechanical or physical things created by man!

Get that clearly fixed in your mind so we may have a common ground upon which to reason out this, the greatest of all questions, "How to Think."

The first thing you do before you start to even plan an advertisement, much less to write it, is to think what you are going to do and how you are going to proceed. If there is no thought, there is no bodily action.

Are we together on that?

Yes, then we will proceed a step further and see if we cannot agree that the success will depend upon the extent to which the thought that goes into it is accurate. If you think accurately and if nothing but facts go into that thought, you will find it comparatively easy to classify and organize those facts. Of course this same logic applies to anything else you might undertake.

THE SUBJECT TO BE THOUGHT ABOUT

The first thing for consideration when you start to think is the subject or object of your thought. It may be the planning of an advertising campaign to be carried out through the leading newspapers of the United States involving an expenditure of $100,000, or it may be the planning of a sales or collection letter, or it may be the planning of a picnic party. There can be no thought without a subject about which to think.

Andrew Carnegie selected the subject of steel manufacture, and, by applying the same principles which we shall explain to you in this lesson, he built up the greatest steel industry in the world and incidentally gained all the success, as measured in dollars, that any man could wish for.

Rockefeller selected the subject of oil about which to think, and, through the application of the same principles, he established the world's greatest oil refining business and made himself a multimillionaire.

James J. Hill selected the subject of railroad building about which to think, and, through application of the same principles, he became the world's greatest railroad builder, even though he didn't start this thinking process until after he was 38 years old.

Orville and Wilbur Wright selected the subject of airplanes about which to think, and they mastered the air and became wealthy in money.

Alexander Graham Bell selected the telephone about which to think, and now we may speak with clearness from New York to San Francisco.

Marconi went a step further and selected the subject of wireless telegraphy about which to think, and now we can communicate with ships in mid-ocean or from coast to coast across the ocean without the use of wires.

The beginning of all these successes was thought – scientific, accurate thought! Furthermore, the process through which these men thought scientifically and accurately was exactly the same in every instance. The same material went into that thought in every case, and the principles underlying it were exactly the same as those which we shall describe for your benefit in this lesson.

"The power to concentrate presupposes the ability to finish all that you start – to stick to everything you undertake with a grim persistence that knows no defeat!"

– Napoleon Hill

The difference between the work done and the results obtained by the men just mentioned, and the work now being done by you and me is chiefly a difference of the subjects selected about which to think and the manner in which the thinking is done. The chances are that you and I can succeed to just as great an extent as did any of these men if we have selected the right subject about which to think and if we think as accurately as these men did.

Those two "ifs" tell the entire story!

It is not the purpose of this lesson to tell you or even suggest what subject you ought to select about which to think, but it is our purpose to show you "How to Think Scientifically and Accurately" on all subjects, whether they be of minor or major importance in relation to your vocation or life's work.

CONCENTRATION

After you have decided upon a subject to which you wish to direct your thought accurately, the next principle of which you must make use is that of Concentration. We will not here go into a thorough scientific explanation of Concentration as that subject is thoroughly explained in subsequent lessons, at the proper time. Our purpose now is to speak of it very briefly as being one of the chief essentials which must be employed in accurate thinking. Concentration is the great highway, so to speak, over which you must transport the other principles which go into accurate thinking. It is the rifle barrel that continues the force of all the other principles into one channel and directs them straight to the bull's eye of the object of your thought.

You can never become an accurate thinker until you have learned to concentrate the forces of your mind and direct them upon one subject until that subject has been mastered.

The power to concentrate presupposes the ability to finish all that you start – to stick to everything you undertake with a grim persistence that knows no defeat!

"Thought without persistent, concentrated bodily action would be useless."

– Napoleon Hill

Concentration means the ability to direct your mind upon a task until it is completed, and you can concentrate upon sharpening a pencil just as well as you can upon becoming a great railroad builder or oil refiner. The principle in each instance is precisely the same.

I must here caution you, however, that unless you form the habit of persistent concentration on the little routine things you do, you will not likely learn how to concentrate upon the bigger things. The extent to which you practice the habit of concentrating upon your routine duties for one day will probably give you an accurate estimate of your ability to concentrate upon the bigger things.

Writing is one of the greatest aids in acquiring the habit of concentration as well as in learning how to organize and classify facts. Thought that is followed with writing is just that much nearer transformation from the mental to the physical state. The architect first thinks, then transfers his "thought" to a blueprint, and from the blueprint the contractor and builder buys the materials and constructs the physical object of the architect's thoughts, which we call a "house."

Writing out our thoughts not only aids concentration, but this bodily, physical action helps us make the first step toward the crystallization of thought into reality. Thought without persistent, concentrated bodily action would be useless.

In classifying your facts, the most important thing is to distinguish between "relevant" and "irrelevant" facts, retaining the former and discarding the latter.

Your subconscious mind builds a mental picture out of the material that you permit to reach it.

Your subconscious mind might be likened to a wax plate. It receives and records all that you permit to reach it through your five senses. It accepts information just as readily as it accepts facts. Bear this in mind in connection with the following underscored paragraph.

Thought which you permit to reach your mind, whether in the nature of facts or mere information, has a tendency to reproduce itself in bodily action.

> "Your mind functions with the thought of material that you supply it. It makes no effort to discriminate. What goes into your mind through your five senses and is there recorded is sure to come out again through the physical, muscular action of your body."

– Napoleon Hill

If you want your mind to function accurately and effectively, then bring about this result by seeing that nothing but facts reach it.

WHAT TO DO AND HOW TO DO IT!

(An after-the-lesson visit with Mr. Hill)

My friend, you have commenced this course and you are going to complete it, primarily because you want to become a master and thereby earn all the money you need for your worldly requirements, but by far the eternal, the biggest, most stupendous fact you will get from this course is a clear understanding of this principle that I have just stated!

When you get this clearly fixed in your mind, that everything physical or mechanical created by mankind must first be created in thought, you will be mighty near the real source, the real cause of all the power you need with which to accomplish anything you desire.

I am so sure that I am guiding you in the right direction that I would write this principle out for you in letters a foot high, on a sheet of pure gold, so it might be more impressive, if I were financially able to do so. I am doing the next best thing by bringing it up for explanation throughout this course, and in that way presenting it to you from every possible angle so you may understand how to make sure of it.

If you want to see some of the results and the wreckage of our inadequate public school system, take a look inside of any prison and you will see them. There is no such thing as "born criminal." People become criminals through ignorance and lack of understanding of the principle I have stated.

Let a child learn when it enters kindergarten and the grade schools that it will become an exact duplicate in bodily action of the thoughts it holds in its mind, and then teach it how to select and hold in that mind the right story of thought material, between the ages of four and twenty, and you may tear down your reform schools and prisons as far as the child is concerned.

It is an everlasting disgrace to humanity that we have left it to sects and denominational institutions such as the Christian Science Church, the New Thought Organizations, and a few others of similar nature to corner the market of knowledge and teach the scientific principles of the mind that are available alike to all of us – the principles which, by the eternal, ought to be taught to all of us before we grow up in ignorance and develop the traits of dishonesty, lack of self-confidence, cynicism, hatred, revenge, skepticism, fear, and the other curses which stand between us and a full and happy life! It is an everlasting indictment against our public school system that the work being done by George Washington Institute is not done in the public schools, where humanity may get ahold on it sooner in life.

This great principle of the human mind which was planted there for our use and enjoyment by the Divine Hand at our birth ought to be shorn of the "occultism" and "mystery" with which it is too often shrouded. It ought to be as well understood as are the principles of arithmetic and grammar, for without it a knowledge of these may serve only the purpose of making a person a more adept criminal.

Give the boys and girls an even break when they leave school by sending them away with a reasonable knowledge concerning the most powerful influence that they have, their own minds, and you will soon see the wealth of the world distribute itself so evenly that it will not be possible for some of us to starve to death amid plenty while others revel in over abundance.

This principle isn't Socialism – it's deeper and more fundamental than Socialism because if the principle I have stated were taught in the public schools and understood by all, it would make Socialism unnecessary and impossible! Instead of dividing up the wealth of the world, distribute the intelligence through which wealth is created (notice I said created, not acquired) and it will stay distributed! Dividing the wealth of the world would do no good without this knowledge because it would soon be right back into the hands of the few who now have it – the few who now understand this principle.

You have grown to maturity and, I sincerely trust, have acquired the qualities of reliability and self-confidence. If you haven't, you will by the time you complete this course. The principles we are teaching will help you yet to succeed and get whatever you want or need in this world, but think of the time you have lost if you haven't understood and been making use of them in the years gone by. Now, by the eternal, through your help, your children will come into a full understanding of these, the greatest of Nature's laws, before they are sent out into the world to learn them by chance. Think of the great advantage that you can give your children in this way.

Cordially your friend,

Napoleon Hill
80 East Randolph St.
Chicago, U.S.A.

G GITOMER'S THOUGHTFUL ACTIONS

HOW TO IMPLEMENT THIS LESSON

Hill starts *Think and Grow Rich* with the timeless statement, "Thoughts are things" – this is insight to the importance that thinking plays in your life, and mine. Hill explains that time, focus, and concentration are the bellwethers of your thought process. The question is: How much "think time" are you allowing yourself? For most it's not enough. Here's what to do… Schedule ten morning minutes each day of thought time, and document your journey. At the end of a year you will have devoted more than 60 full hours to personal thought time. I'll bet there's a usable idea or two in there someplace.

"You may be wealthy for all I know, that isn't SUCCESS! You may have a splendid education for all I know, but that isn't success either! You may have wealthy parents, but neither is that SUCCESS, for you must remember that wealth, as measured in dollars and cents, is an evasive thing which sometimes takes wings and flies away. The only real, permanent, and worthwhile SUCCESS is represented by the character you are building."

– Napoleon Hill

Lesson Number

IMAGINATION

[G] GITOMER INSIGHT: Ever get a great idea? Ever daydream? Of course you have. This lesson provides insightful information about HOW and WHY ideas and creativity happen. The insight contained here will give you incentive and inspiration to begin generating both self-improvement ideas AND money generating ideas. Imagine that...

In this lesson, you are taking up one of the most important subjects covered in the fundamentals of living and success – Imagination.

Imagination is held by your instructors to be the most important subject in connection with your education.

Imagination – worlds of it – is one of man's most useful qualifications; the more he has of it, the better. Just as Dr. Hess says, "The man with imagination is he who has visions of a world to come and whose influence repopulates and builds anew the earth."

Thoroughly absorb that statement! Study deeply, ponder over, and fully realize what that sentence means! Give just as close attention to the other valuable thoughts presented by Dr. Hess in this lesson; master them! Then you will know the importance of Imagination to your success.

It is impossible for any student to give this subject too much study. Without a complete knowledge of the principles of Imagination and their application to work, you cannot have the firm grounding in fundamentals that you need for a well-rounded education.

The big places in all walks of life today go to the men of ideas, the men who are able to think constructively, and from time immemorial the great thinkers have been the well-read men – the men who have profited by the study and experience of those who went before them.

To be successful, you must be able to plan and think, and it is the aim and ambition of your instructors to teach you this above all else – to plan and to think.

I want you to become the architect who conceives the structure in heart and brain and then places a picture of it on paper. I do not want you to become the carpenter, the man who executes the plans of the architect. The reason for this is obvious: the architect, the man who plans, probably makes $10,000 a year, whereas the man who executes the plan generally draws around five dollars a day at his limit.

> **G** **GITOMER NOTE: Keep in mind this is in dollars from 1917– $10,000 in today's dollars would be approximately $150,000, and $5.00 a day back then is about $80.00 today.**

You bet it takes energy and imagination to do the exceptional thing, and the man who hesitates because of lack of self-confidence, to put into operation a sales situation or campaign because the plan isn't new and original, might as well quit before starting.

GET MORE INFO NOW: According to Hill, "The Advertiser's Imagination" is vitally important and should be read and studied a dozen times. It's taken from a book called *Productive Advertising* written in 1915 by Herbert Hess – find it here: HillsFirstWritings.com.

That you may more fully appreciate the value of Imagination, read the following editorial, written by Bruce Barton, appearing in *Every Week* magazine. This is an editorial which no student of life and success can afford to miss. But – do not content yourself with reading this editorial only once; go over it again and again until you have thoroughly assimilated the big thought on the back of it. Here it is:

"SOME POOR BLIND FOOLS HAVE NEVER SEEN A MIRACLE."

(Note: The author is not making a reference to physical blindness.)

Here is an important distinction that many people overlook:

God made THE world; but He doesn't make YOUR world.

He provides the raw materials, and out of them every man selects what he wants and builds an individual world for himself.

The fool looks over the wealth of material provided, and selects a few plates of ham and eggs, a few pairs of trousers, a few dollar bills – and is satisfied.

The wise man builds his world out of wonderful sunsets, and thrilling experiences, and the song of the stars, and romance and miracles.

Nothing wonderful ever happens in the life of the fool.

"A primrose by the river's brim A yellow primrose was to him, and it was nothing more"; an electric light is simply an electric light; a telephone is only a telephone – nothing unusual at all.

But the wise man never ceases to wonder how a tiny speck of seed, apparently dead and buried, can produce a beautiful yellow flower.

He never lifts the telephone receiver or switches on an electric light without a certain feeling of awe.

And think what a miracle it is, this harnessing of electricity to the service of man!

Who, unless his sense of awe has grown blunt through constant familiarity, would believe it?

The sun, the center of our universe, goes down behind the western horizon. I touch a button and presto! I have called it back again – the room is flooded again with light.

The thunder that men once called the voice of God rolls out its mighty waves of sound, and the sound carries only a few score miles. But I – puny speck upon the face of the earth – I lift a little instrument and, behold, my whisper is heard a thousand miles away.

Prometheus stole fire from the gods and brought it down to earth. And for that crime the gods chained him to a lonely rock and sent a huge bird to tear out his vitals. Each night the wound healed, and each day it was torn open again.

That was the punishment of the man who dared to wrest away the richest treasure of the gods.

But fire – the treasure of the gods – has almost disappeared out of our daily life; we scorn it.

Do we want heat? We press a button and lo, heat invisible, silent, all-pervasive, flows into our homes over a copper wire.

DO we need power? We have but to press another switch, and giants come to us over the same slender roadway. Clothed in invincible garments, they cleanse our homes, wash our clothes, crank our automobiles – do everything that once taxed the strength of men and hurried women into old age.

Don't let your life become a prosaic affair; don't let familiarity with the marvels about you breed thoughtlessness and contempt.

Let the fool build his world out of mere food and drink and clothes! You fashion yours out of marvelous experiences; furnish and decorate it with miracles!

Exercise your mind in the wholesome activity of wonder; train your soul to reverent awe.

If you had stood with Moses at the shore of the Red Sea, and had seen it divide to let the children of Israel pass over, you would have had no difficulty in recognizing that as a miracle.

But every night when the sun goes down, a man stands in a power house in your city and throws a switch, and instantly the city and the country for miles around are flooded with sunshine.

And you say to yourself casually, "Oh, I see the lights are on!"

— Bruce Barton, Editor.

GITOMER NOTE: The author is saying that if things are taken for granted, and assumed to be there for us to indulge in, then imagination and its sister creativity will be stifled. Take a close look at the examples of heat and electricity – they were NEW! Obviously society and technology have taken several quantum leaps – BUT this is an individual challenge to YOU – where is YOUR imagination and creativity? How are you discovering it and using it for personal and universal benefit? Or are you still (100 years later) just turning on the lights?

The following letter, written by Mr. Hill, presents another concrete example of the use of imagination:

DEAR FRIEND,

I went back for a visit to the old farm this past summer. It was the first time I had been there in twenty years.

You'd be surprised to know how things had changed. The old swimming hole that used to be so deep that it was supposed not to have any bottom was filled up with sand. Trees have grown up around the banks and the old river didn't look as it did twenty years ago when I was learning to swim on a rail.

The old farm showed signs of better days, and the old home was weather beaten and dilapidated. No one knew me. The chums of my boyhood days had grown up and moved away. New faces and strange people looked at me askance. The dogs barked at me.

For the first time in my life I felt like Rip Van Winkle. What a forlorn feeling that is! I can't describe it to you. You would have to feel that way yourself to understand it.

The little cedar tree, which I planted twenty-five years ago, had grown to be the largest tree on the place. It was a little sprig of branches not more than a foot high when I planted it.

I met a boy bringing the cows home from the pasture. He had a fishing pole on his shoulder. His face was berry-stained. His trousers struck him at the ankles and were two sizes too big. There was a big patch on the seat and one on each knee. One suspender held them up. The front end of that suspender was fastened to a wooden peg instead of a button. He was barefooted. He grinned at me sheepishly. I knew where he got that berry-stained face for I had slipped into Sid Well's berry patch many a time myself. But I loved the looks of that sunburned boy. He looked just as I did some twenty years ago. We stopped and looked each other over. We didn't say anything, but we understood. He could tell by the expression on my face that I was his kind.

The only person I met who recognized me was my old sweetheart. We used to go to school together when I wore knickerbockers and she wore knee dresses and sunbonnets. She was married. Four little dirty faces peeped out from behind her skirt and eyed me suspiciously. I took out my watch and showed her the picture of my wife and two boys. We had a pleasant little chat. Her husband came in from the harvest fields. He was a sturdy young chap, but he didn't seem to take to me very well. I had my suspicions why.

I stopped at the old sulphur spring for a drink of water. As I lifted the gourd cup to my parched lips, I thought of those good old days of long ago, when I carried water from that same old spring in a tin bucket. I sat down on the rock wall that protects the spring from surface water and had a half hour's pleasant visit in the realms of the past. It was like a dream. Everything came back to me so vividly, so real. The strong smell of sulphur water, the pine needles drifting down from the spring, the smell of the new-mown hay from the nearby meadow carried me back to the days of my childhood.

Step by step I retraced my past. In that short half hour I lived it all over again. My first thought was of my mother, who died when I was nine years old. Then all the memories of things that were unpleasant – of a battle for existence that has been contested at every stop – a battle that began the day I was deprived of my home.

Then came the unpleasant and ghost-like memories of those long days and nights that followed which I spent in the wilderness, with no roof over my head, no home, no friends.

Then came the memories of my first job, chopping Spanish needles with a goose-neck hoe in return for my board. Then my new job in a coal mine at a dollar a day. My! That was a lot of money – a whole dollar for a day's work!

Then more pleasant memories led me over my later experiences, from the day I got my first position as a stenographer to the day that I graduated in law. Then came still more pleasant memories of the day I became Assistant to the Chief Counsel for one of the largest companies in the world at a salary of $2,500 a year – the same company that owned the coal mine where I had worked at a dollar a day. Another shift in the memories of the past brought me back to the day I became advertising manager for one of the largest institutions of its kind in the world, at a salary of $5,000 a year.

I was startled as if coming out of a trance. It was just like living over the past twenty years. A cold perspiration stood on my forehead. The joys and sorrows of the past had all swept over me again, as realistic as they were when I first experienced them.

I visited the little white schoolhouse on the top of the hill, two miles away, where I first went to school. The same old schoolhouse, with the same old benches, was right there, all carved up and marked with initials just like they were twenty years ago. I played with the school children during the noon hour. We played a game of baseball and also had a turn at "bull pen." Then the school bell rang. The teacher was a young girl who wasn't born when I was down in that country last. She let me "teach" for half an hour. I had the time of my life, and so did the boys and girls.

We mixed mirth with melody. I told them some funny stories, and then I wound up by telling them about the day I left that country, and about some of my experiences since that day. I saw a good many dampened eyelids in the room. I'm not so sure that my own eyes were exactly dry.

I wrote a few lines of "shorthand" on the blackboard. Not one of them had ever heard of shorthand. Not one of them had so much as thought about what he or she was going to do to earn a living. Some of them were old enough to begin thinking seriously about this, too.

Poor little fellows! I hardly knew whether to pity them or congratulate them at first, but after I got back to the city and began to think it over, I came to the conclusion that I ought to pity them for being placed in an environment like that.

A little adversity is good for us! The man to be really pitied is the fellow who grows up with a "silver spoon" in his mouth, with a rich dad and no responsibilities! It's a safe ten-to-one shot that such a man will never be a very strong competitor of the fellow who has had to fight hard for every foot of ground he has covered in his life's progress.

It is not wealth that makes a man – it is character, persistence, and a strong determination to be of service to the world! Don't forget that word S-E-R-V-I-C-E! If you ever succeed in life, you may rest assured that your real success will be measured and determined by the QUANTITY and QUALITY of the SERVICE you render.

You may be wealthy for all I know; that isn't SUCCESS! You may have a splendid education for all I know, but that isn't success either! You may have wealthy parents, but neither is that SUCCESS, for you must remember that wealth, as measured in dollars and cents, is an evasive thing which sometimes takes wings and flies away. The only real, permanent, and worthwhile SUCCESS is represented by the character you are building.

> **Ğ** **GITOMER NOTE: Take a moment to think about your character and how important it is to your success. Do a realistic self-assessment and write areas for improvements as well as those elements you believe are excellent. Make a definite plan to improve and strengthen your character.**

And remember that whether you know it or not, you are building some sort of character all the time. The chances are ten to one that if you are devoting some of your time to self-improvement through the reading of the right sort of books, you are building a character that will be an asset to you in years to come. On the other hand, the odds are just as great that if you are squandering your time in idle amusement, and giving no thought to self-improvement, your character will not be improved, but may become an embarrassing liability in the years to come.

Character is built slowly, step by step. Your every thought and every action go into it.

James Allen truly said: "AS A MAN THINKETH SO IS HE!" If you think worthwhile things, you are pretty apt to be a worthwhile man. You can be pretty much whatever you want to be. If you want to be a Mechanical Engineer, or an Electrical Engineer, or an Expert Accountant, or a Stenographer or a Lawyer, or an Advertising Manager, or anything else, you CAN if you keep your mind on that one thing.

We should never complain if success does not come easily. If it did, we might not recognize it when it arrived!

My sympathies and my best wishes are with you, whether I hear from you or not, but I cannot be of much help to you unless you take me into your confidence and tell me frankly what you are up against. Is there anything you would like to ask the College to do for you?

Whatever you may undertake in life, whatever your lot may be, whether you are successful or unsuccessful, rich or poor, just remember that I am ever ready to extend to you the hand of good fellowship. And also remember that if you ever happen to come to Chicago, there is a warm welcome awaiting you here at the College.

With all good wishes for your success, believe me.

Cordially and sincerely yours,

Napoleon Hill

Napoleon Hill

"The only real, permanent and worthwhile SUCCESS is represented by the character you are building."

– Napoleon Hill

IMPORTANT NOTES on IMAGINATION and WRITING

By way of explanation we will add that Mr. Hill did not make the trip back to the old home place, which he describes in this letter. It is all his idea of what might have happened had he made this trip.

This letter is presented not only as a concrete illustration of the practical use of Imagination, but also as an example of the effectiveness of short, terse sentences. Notice the simplicity of the words used and how easy it is to follow the writer of the letter. You find no involved, long, drawn-out sentences. This is the most effective style to use in writing sales literature of any kind, and you must aim constantly to develop this style if you are to write business-getting information.

Then, too, there is another good lesson in this letter. It was written as part of a follow-up system for correspondence school in which Mr. Hill was interested. You may be interested to know that while this letter says very little about "selling a correspondence course," it brought back over $50,000 in business. The evident sincerity back of the letter, the human interest of the entire story, the simplicity of the words employed, all formed a powerful selling influence.

Mr. J. F. Stevens of our staff presents the following treatise on the subject of Imagination from a more practical viewpoint than that of Dr. Hess. He discusses the subject as follows:

Although your textbook divides Imagination into six kinds of classes, you will find a two-fold division sufficient for practical use. This two-fold division is: First, Reproductive Imagination; second, Productive Imagination.

By the power of Reproductive Imagination, you reproduce or reconstruct in your mind a picture or mental image of a previous experience. Can you imagine just how the dinner table looked yesterday? Try! What food was on the table? How did it taste? Was the odor of cooking savory? What was the conversation about? Do you recall the touch of your knife and fork, your napkin and the dishes, as you handled them?

"Character is built slowly, step by step. Your every thought and every action go into it."

– *Napoleon Hill*

The picture you get of the dinner table is an example of Reproductive Imagination. You have created nothing new. You have simply recalled, as it occurred, a previous experience.

Productive Imagination, on the other hand, takes elements or parts of previous experiences and combines them in a new, novel, or fantastic way.

Let us see how! Picture an instrument that permits you to look through buildings and mountains as though they were thin air; that enables you to glimpse at will the sandy stretches of the Sahara Desert, or the battlefields of Europe; that brings everything everywhere within the range of your eye. Your mental image of this instrument is an example of Productive Imagination. Have you, however, created anything new?

We will dissolve this product of the imagination into its elements and see if it is not a combination of parts of previous experiences. First, there is the idea of transparency. That is nothing new. We have all explained the transparency of glass. We have all heard of the X-ray which makes hidden things visible. Second, there is the idea of drawing distant places near so that we can see them clearly. That is not a new idea. We are familiar with the telescope or opera glass. Consequently, you see that our fantastic example of Productive Imagination is, in truth, merely a putting-together of fragments of previous experiences in a new combination.

You will find that you are unable, even with the help of the wonderful instrument we have imagined, to picture any place, landscape, or thing that you have not seen either in person or in pictures.

You can re-create in your mind only those impressions or experiences which have come to you through your senses. A blind person cannot imagine an aeroplane in flight because he has never seen one flying, not even a picture of one. He can tell how it feels if he has gone over it with his fingers. A deaf person cannot imagine the sound of church bells because he has never heard them. If he has seen them, he can picture their appearance.

In Imagination, therefore, you can only picture, in whole or in part, those things which you have seen, heard, felt, smelt, or tasted.

You will find ample opportunities to employ both Reproductive and Productive Imagination.

Fix this firmly – there can be nothing in the mind that has not come in through the senses. Therefore, keep your appeal to the imagination in terms of your past experiences.

If you reflect, you will note that there is a distinct type of Imagination for each sense. We will classify these as follows:

SENSE:	*TYPE OF IMAGERY:*
Hearing.	*Auditory imagery*
Seeing	*Visual imagery*
Feeling	*Muscular imagery*
Tasting	*Gustatory imagery*
Smelling	*Olfactory imagery*

Sometimes an image is a blending of several types. Thus, your mental picture of a cup of coffee may be a composite of its appearance, its taste, and its aroma.

There are then five important things to remember about Imagination:

First: That for practical purposes it is of two kinds:

(a) Reproductive Imagination

(b) Productive Imagination

Second: That imagination can only reproduce or combine sense experiences.

Third: That the appeal to the imagination is limited by the extent of past experiences.

Fourth: That there should be an appropriate relation between the image and the type of imagery appealed to.

Fifth: The question is often asked in connection with this lesson: How can I develop my Imagination for practical use?"

It can be done, and is being done all around us every day:

First, by reading, observation, and study of men and things;

Second, by the use of memory, storing the results of our study in our minds, and recalling them when needed;

Third, by fitting our previous experiences and knowledge to the conditions of others.

It is well for you to strengthen your Imagination from both Literature and Life. Certain reading is very beneficial to the development of Imagination.

There are certain characters in literature that become as real and impressive to us as the members of our own family, and we see the results of the Imagination of the author. Take the characters of Dickens, for example – Mr. Pickwick, Nicholas Nickleby, Oliver Twist, the Parish Beadle, Old Fagin, the Artful Dodger, Nancy, and Bill Sikes. Or those of Robert Louis Stevenson; or of Kipling; Sherlock Holmes, as imagined by Conan Doyle; or the Chicago street boy, Artie, by George Ade; and the ball player, depicted by Ring Lardner's *You Know Me, Al.* All are splendid works of the Imagination and well worthy of study, because they truly depict human life under varying conditions and will increase one's knowledge of the world.

In the realm of science, Imagination plays its part. Jules Verne saw the submarine in Imagination, though *Twenty Thousand Leagues Under the Sea* seemed impossible of realization, if not ridiculous, to the readers of his day. So with the airplane, which Langley, Chanute, and the Wright brothers not only saw first in Imagination, but lived to realize.

Akin to these imaginary characters of Literature are the imaginary characters in Advertising, products of the same mental faculty. Take the faces of "Before and After" ads, and you see the images clearly.

Art lives and thrives on the Imagination of the true artist, and artists are lending themselves more and more to the aid of commerce, so that there is real art in much of the advertising today. Men and women should at least keep up with the artist in the matter of fruitful Imagination.

While Imagination is not always to be given free rein, it will be found highly desirable from time to time. So, cultivate your Imagination and make it work for you! Like all other faculties, you will find it a poor master, but a good servant.

> ## "Never complain if success does not come easily. If it did, you might not recognize it when it arrived!"
>
> ### – Napoleon Hill

𝖌 GITOMER'S THOUGHTFUL ACTIONS

HOW TO IMPLEMENT THIS LESSON

Think about the most successful ideas you have ever had. Then put together the scenario that created the idea. The place, the people, the surroundings, the time, and your situation in life at that moment. Those same elements will help you understand how to create new ideas. When you get an idea, you might want to run it by your trusted advisors or mentors first. People who will give you honest feedback. Then run it by a few friends – if they say, "You're nuts," I promise you are on the right path. Just ask the people who thought Steve Jobs or Bill Gates or Jeff Bezos were nuts.

"Effort only fully releases its reward after a person refuses to quit."

– Napoleon Hill

Lesson Number

5

THE VALUE OF SELF-CONFIDENCE AND SINCERITY

(An after-the-lesson visit with Mr. Hill)

G GITOMER INSIGHT: Hill tells you verbally and visually what it takes (with examples) to become a self-confident person. And what happens after you become one. The secret weapon is how sincere you are both in swagger and conversation.

"Lo! A scoffer remains to pray!"

The above is the first sentence in a letter that I received with an enrollment from a new student.

This student frankly admitted, in this letter, that he wrote to us out of curiosity, having no intention whatsoever at the time of becoming a student.

He has been in business several years, and felt that he already knew enough, so he said. He commences to get letters from me. There was something about them, he couldn't tell just what, that appealed to him. For one thing he knew that I was SINCERE! That I was really and truly interested in my students!

This is but one of many hundred similar instances where students have expressed themselves about as this man did. I mention this only for the purpose – to prelude what I am going to write about the value of sincerity in everything we write.

Sincerity cannot be feigned!

If it is real, your readers will feel that it is, just as this man did. If it is unreal, they will likewise feel it. Words, written or spoken, that come from the brain instead of the heart will not convince. Try as you may, if you do not believe what you write or speak, others will not believe it!

Words that are not backed by sincerity have inhibitory and negative effect!

> **G GITOMER NOTE: Think about your own sincerity. How genuine it is, and how easy it is for you to spot insincerity in others. And it doesn't matter if you think you're sincere. The only opinion that matters is that of the other person.**

I have been asked, hundreds of times, how to learn to write "human interest" letters. This has always been an embarrassing question to me, not because I didn't know what to say, but because I didn't know HOW TO SAY IT SO IT WOULD BE UNDERSTOOD!

Some people believe that an inspirational writer is only born with that ability. Nothing could be further from the truth, in my opinion.

> **G GITOMER NOTE: As a "how-to, informational, and inspirational writer" for the past 25 years, I can tell without a shadow of a doubt that Hill is correct. I was born with intelligence, but I learned to write. Same with sales. Same with public speaking.**

Others believe that a thorough understanding of English is all that is necessary. Neither is that true! It is a well-known fact that not more than one out of a hundred teachers of English can write an inspirational appeal. Teaching the emotions through the use of words depends upon what is in the heart and not upon what is in the brain.

Take that wonderful speech which Lincoln delivered at Gettysburg. It was short. The words were very simple. But you cannot read them without feeling a strong touch of emotion. These words have retained the sincerity which was back of them when they were uttered. Notice how they touch your heart as you read:

"Four score and seven years ago our fathers brought forth on this continent, a new nation, conceived in Liberty, and dedicated to the proposition that all men are created equal.

"Now we are engaged in a great civil war, testing whether that nation, or any nation so conceived and so dedicated, can long endure. We have met on a great battle-field of that war. We have come to dedicate a portion of that field, as a final resting place for those who here gave their lives that that nation might live. It is altogether fitting and proper that we should do this.

"But, in a larger sense, we can not dedicate – we can not consecrate – we can not hallow – this ground. The brave men, living and dead, who struggled here, have consecrated it, far above our poor power to add or detract. The world will little note, nor long remember what we say here, but it can never forget what they did here. It is for us the living, rather, to be dedicated here to the unfinished work which they who fought here have thus far so nobly advanced. It is rather for us to be here dedicated to the great task remaining before us – that from these honored dead we take increased devotion to that cause for which they gave the last full measure of devotion – that we here highly resolve that these dead shall not have died in vain – that this nation, under God, shall have a new birth of freedom – and that government of the people, by the people, for the people, shall not perish from the earth."

Whatever field of work you enter, it is necessary for you to learn to write convincing appeals. Your success will largely depend upon the logic, emotion, and the sincerity of your appeals. Let me leave this thought with you…

YOUR READERS AND ASSOCIATES WILL ALWAYS "SENSE"
YOUR APPEALS, WHETHER THEY ARE CONSCIOUS OF
THAT FACT OR NOT! BE CAREFUL THEN, TO SEE THAT
EVERY STATEMENT YOU SEND OUT IS BACKED WITH
YOUR WHOLE-HEARTED BELIEF IN WHAT YOU WRITE!

Let no sum of money tempt you to write anything that you do not
believe! It is a bad habit to get into. It will take away that finer inner-
self which you ought to develop and bring out.

When a person asks me how I learned to write "human interest"
letters, I always do my best to explain that my outward expression is
but a duplicate of my inner feelings! That my letters are based upon
what is in my heart!

Beginners and those who are inexperienced usually feel that my
explanation is inadequate. This does not surprise me. If a person had
made the same explanation to me fifteen years ago, I wouldn't have
understood it either.

As you go further into this course and learn more about the workings
of the human mind – as you learn to study human nature more
closely – you will say just what I am saying now. You have possibly
reached that state of understanding already. If so, I congratulate you.

My students all seem to feel, just as the "scoffer who remained to
pray" did, that there is sincerity back of my letters to them. Many of
them have expressed their willingness to give anything they possess to
be able to write as well as I do.

Let me assure you now, once and for all, that there is no secret to
this except that which I have explained. Your true feelings always will
show in your writing. If you are not satisfied with your writing ability,
go back to the first class. Your own heart and your own emotions hold
the secret. If you want to write a letter that will appeal to a certain
person and gain his confidence, first think well of that person and
give him or her your own confidence.

If you want to write a letter that will appeal to a certain class of people, first put yourself in their place – study their environment – become sympathetic with them – study their requirements – then study the product you are going to try to sell and see just how it fits the needs of those people.

No actor ever moved an audience who did not himself experience the emotional feelings that he was trying to produce in his audience.

You cannot win the FULL confidence of a person you do not admire. There will always be an invisible barrier as long as you permit any feeling of dislike to exist, even though no outward appearance of it may be noticed.

Hate your employer and he, probably unconsciously, will get your thought vibrations, and retaliate in kind! Distrust your fellow men and they, in turn, will distrust you – not openly, perhaps, but none-the-less effectively!

Your thoughts bring back their likeness to curse or bless you, according to their kind!

There is nothing mystic or occult about this.

It is a scientific law of nature! A law that we shall have more to say about later on in this course.

Thoughts are wonderful things! Keep them clean and they will draw people to you. Let them stray in the wrong direction and they will repulse worthwhile people, even though they are never expressed through words, written or spoken.

> **G GITOMER NOTE:** The first words in *Think and Grow Rich* are "Thoughts are things." Here they appear for the first time, 20 years before being immortalized.

One of my best friends stood behind me, looking over my shoulder, as I was writing one night. This was a very impolite thing to do, but imagine my consternation when she said: "I DON'T LIKE THAT – I DON'T BELIEVE THE MAGAZINE WILL ACCEPT IT!"

I seldom turn my tongue loose on anyone, although I may sometimes allow my thoughts to wander around in unwholesome places, but on this occasion, I said things which both of us will not soon forget.

I had never preached a sermon before, but I preached one then!

Luckily for us both, that occurrence kept my friend from becoming my wife! Imagine being wedded to a woman who would look over your shoulder, anticipate your words even before they had been written, and tell you that she didn't like what you were writing, and that she didn't believe others would like it either!

Not one man out of ten thousand could rise above a negative environment such as that and overcome its inhibitory effects.

It is both a physiological and a psychological case that causes us to respond readily to suggestion. Let us take care then to guard carefully the suggestions which reach our minds, and to see that they are of a constructive nature!

You cannot think of failure constantly and be a success!

"You will be just what you think you will be" not all at one jump, understand, but slowly, step by step, your thoughts crystallize into action, and out of this action grows your material world, good or bad!

No man can hide his real self for long! The real you is written in your face as well as in your actions. Some people believe that because they are met with warm greetings that they are trusted. Many a man, for politeness' sake, is cordial in his outward expression, yet very skeptical and distrustful inwardly.

I feel reasonably sure you agree with me in all that I have written in this "visit." However, I can hear you ask: "How may I develop these desirable qualities of which you write?"

That is an important question, I'll admit.

Well, I will answer it by giving you lesson number one in SELF-CONFIDENCE, for without self-confidence you cannot hope to develop the other desirable qualities that you will need as an aid to success in any field of endeavor.

Following is lesson number one in the art of developing self-confidence. Sign it and then proceed to commit it to memory. There is a scientific reason for this request – a reason that I shall tell you more of at the proper time. In these seven short paragraphs you may find all of the philosophy necessary for your success in any undertaking:

SELF-CONFIDENCE-BUILDING CHART

(To be memorized and recited daily)

(1) I know that I have the ability to accomplish all that I undertake – that to succeed I only have to follow this belief in myself with vigorous, aggressive action! I WILL FOLLOW IT!

(2) I realize that my thoughts reproduce themselves in the material, physical state, therefore I will concentrate upon the daily task of drawing the mental picture of the person I intend to be, and of transforming this picture into reality.

(3) I am studying Life and Salesmanship with the firm intention of mastering the fundamentals and principles through which I may attract to me the desirable things of life. Through this study I am becoming more self-reliant, more cheerful, more sympathetic with my fellow men and stronger both mentally and physically. I am learning to smile the smile that plays upon the heart as well as upon the lips.

"'You will be just what you think you will be' not all at one jump, understand, but slowly, step by step, your thoughts crystallize into action, and out of this action grows your material world, good or bad!"

— Napoleon Hill

(4) I am mastering overpowering the habit of starting something that I do not finish! From this time forward I will first plan all that I wish to do, making a clear mental picture of it, and then I will let nothing interfere with my plans until they have been developed into reality.

(5) I have clearly mapped out and planned the work that I intend to follow for the ensuing five years. I have set a price upon my services for each of these five years – a price that I INTEND TO COMMAND THROUGH STRICT APPLICATION OF THE PRINCIPLE OF EFFICIENT, SATISFACTORY SERVICE!

(6) I fully realize that GENUINE SUCCESS will come only through strict application of the "Golden Rule" principle. I will therefore engage in no transaction which does not benefit alike all who participate with me. I will succeed by attracting to me the forces that I wish to use. I will induce others to serve me because of my willingness to serve them. I will gain the friendship of my fellow men because of my kindness and my willingness to be a friend. I will eliminate from my mind FEAR by developing in its place COURAGE. I will eliminate skepticism by developing FAITH. I will eliminate hatred and cynicism by developing love for humanity.

(7) I will learn to stand upon my feet and express myself in clear, concise, and simple language, and to speak with force and enthusiasm, in a manner that will carry conviction. I will cause others to become interested in me because I will first become interested in them. I will eliminate SELFISHNESS and develop in its place the spirit of SERVICE, as taught by the George Washington Institute.

Sign _____

Your earnest friend,

Napoleon Hill

80 East Randolph St.
Chicago, U.S.A.

📷 GITOMER'S THOUGHTFUL ACTIONS

HOW TO IMPLEMENT THIS LESSON

Self-belief leads to self-confidence. It starts in your head and heart way before you can manifest it to others. And in today's world, self-confidence is manifest in BOTH speaking and writing. The Internet and social media has provided unlimited platforms of expression, and search engines have created instant ways for the world to discover your thoughts. The key to speaking is your ability to engage emotionally. The key to writing and achieving is self-belief and clarity of thought. This also means not accepting "criticism" with anything but a "thank you" in response. Belief that what you say, do, or write about is from your heart, not just your head. Your internal belief. If you doubt anything said in these golden words and thoughts, keep in mind that Napoleon Hill has sold MORE THAN 100 million books, and you haven't (neither have I).

"For without self-confidence you cannot hope to develop the other desirable qualities that you will need as an aid to success in any field of endeavor."

– Napoleon Hill

"Affirmations: Any idea, plan, or purpose may be placed in the mind through repetition of thought."

— Napoleon Hill

Lesson Number

LET AMBITION BE YOUR MASTER

(An after-the-lesson visit with Mr. Hill)

G GITOMER INSIGHT: Everyone has a big goal and a dream of who they seek to become and what they hope to achieve or get. Hill uncovers the "inside your head" element that will drive you to success: AMBITION. His definitions will startle you, and lead you on a path to success. Your success.

LUCKY is the man who is driven by that determined little slave master called AMBITION! Those who have enjoyed the greatest success in life were literally driven to succeed by AMBITION. It made Harriman, Rockefeller, Carnegie, Hill, Roosevelt, and a good many thousands of other successful men of whom we never hear.

Ambition is the mainspring of life, but we must keep it wound up! Self-confidence is the balance wheel which keeps ambition moving at an even momentum. Enthusiasm is the oil with which we keep the human machine greased and in smooth running order. The well-organized, capable, and productive man is AMBITIOUS, ENTHUSIASTIC, and possesses plenty of SELF-CONFIDENCE. Without these, success is uncertain, if not impossible.

The chief reason that I consent to my wife going back to the farm every summer is that while she is away, she constantly writes me letters which fire me with AMBITION! She understands me as few wives understand their husbands. She knows how necessary it is to constantly remind me of my chief aims in life, and she has a way of doing it which is pleasing and inspiring.

When I secured my first $5,000-a-year position, I thought I was fixed for life, and probably I would have been had it not been for that little master for whom I was slaving – AMBITION! My wife and AMBITION collaborated against me and made me resign that position – FOR A BIGGER ONE! Five thousand a year would have satisfied me had it not been for my master, AMBITION. In my bigger and broader field I serve a hundred of my fellow men where I served one before, which means that I get a hundred times as much enjoyment out of life as well as financial returns, which are adequate and in proportion to the service which I perform.

AMBITION is what freed America from over-the-sea rulership.

Once in my life, while I was working for a salary, I was discharged from my position – just ONCE! The head of the institution for which I worked told me that I was too "ambitious." That was the greatest compliment anyone ever paid me, even though it cut me off temporarily from my bread and meat.

That institution of which I write was organized nearly twenty years ago. It is doing a business of about $600,000 a year.[*1] Another institution, engaged in the same line of business, started just six years ago on capital of less than $6,000.[*2] I was formerly Advertising Manager of this institution. It does not discourage "AMBITION." It is now doing a business of $1,500,000[*3] a year, and clearing more net profits every month than the other firm is doing in gross business. The older institution, the one which was organized and has been doing

[*1] $600,000 equals $8,800,000 today.

[*2] $6,000 equals $88,000 today.

[*3] $1,500,000 equals $22,000,000 today.

business for nearly twenty years, is headed by men who are afraid of the "AMBITIOUS MAN." Those who are working for a salary are afraid he will get their jobs (which said fear is not without some foundation). The head of the firm is afraid of the "AMBITIOUS MAN" because he is afraid he will find in him a competitor in business (which, also, is not without well-grounded foundation).

BUT – AND HERE IS THE CRUX OF MY WHOLE STORY OF THESE TWO FIRMS – THE MAJORITY OF BUSINESS FIRMS ARE LOOKING FOR MEN WHO HAVE PLENTY OF "AMBITION." Do not worry because one firm is afraid of the ambitious man. The very fact that such a firm is afraid of him is, in itself, strong evidence of weakness on the part of those who manage the firm.

While I was Advertising Manager of the younger firm of which I have written, I had three young men in my department. I put them on notice that someday one of them would get my position, and I commenced training them for my job. I told them that the man who "made good" first would get the place, if my recommendations would help any. My Secretary landed the prize. He is still with that firm, making more money than the average man of his age receives. I did not discourage "AMBITION" for fear of losing my job. I encouraged it so that someone would grow to be big enough to push me out of the rut and into a bigger position. That is what happened. I have no patience to speak of with the man who is so narrow that he is afraid to inspire "AMBITION" in his fellow workers. Show me a man who believes he has a corner on the details connected with his job and I will show you, in the same person, a man who will never develop beyond petty selfishness.

I beseech you not to fall into the habit of neglecting to cultivate your "AMBITION." You will need something more than mere services with which to succeed. You will need that ever-alert little matter which is the subject of this lesson. But, I must here give you a word of warning – do not let your ambition become a selfish one! The greatest object over which to develop ambition is the desire to serve our fellow men. We cannot serve them if we are jealous of them.

Remember, also, that AMBITION is a contagious thing. If you give it to the world, the world will give it back to you in increased measure. But keep it unto yourself and you will lose it. It will take wings and fly!

Ambition finds expression in a thousand different forms. It is the foundation which underlies all invention, art, music, industry, commerce – nay, the very foundation upon which the progress of the world has been built. Within the present generation, we have seen it expressed in the most wonderful inventions the world has ever known; the automobile, the telephone, the wireless, the submarine, the X-ray, and the aeroplane.

AMBITION was the very warp and woof out of which these things were constructed. Ambition leads us to think, and when we begin to think, the nebulous problems in the world's evolution begin to become clarified and simplified. BE AMBITIOUS IF NOTHING MORE. OTHER THINGS WILL TAKE CARE OF THEMSELVES.

Your earnest friend,

Napoleon Hill

80 East Randolph St.
Chicago, U.S.A.

G GITOMER'S THOUGHTFUL ACTIONS

HOW TO IMPLEMENT THIS LESSON

The key to Ambition is personal drive tied to attitude, self-belief, and determination to succeed – NO MATTER WHAT. The good news is that most people do NOT possess this formula. You now have it and the wisdom to boot. Substitute the examples that Hill offers for your own ambitions. Put a few Post-it® notes on your bathroom mirror as both a reminder and inspiration to "never, never, never give up" (Winston Churchill). You are the master of your fate, and the captain of the team to achieve your dreams.

"AMBITION is a contagious thing."

— Napoleon Hill

"If you give it to the world, the world will give it back to you in increased measure. But keep it unto yourself and you will lose it. It will take wings and fly!"

— *Napoleon Hill*

"Education comes from within; you get it by struggle and effort and thought."

— *Napoleon Hill*

Lesson Number

7

ADVERSITY: A BLESSING IN DISGUISE

(An after-the-lesson visit with Mr. Hill)

G GITOMER INSIGHT: When it all goes wrong…
At the end of failure is the beginning of success, but
most people are wallowing deep in self-pity and anger,
and fail to see the Golden Ticket right in front of their
face. It's up to YOU and your self-determination to get
it going again. Hill's positive perspective on adversity
will give you hope and answers to whatever befalls you
on your way to success. Read to succeed.

Friend, do not become discouraged, disappointed, and disheartened
if the seemingly cruel hand of fate knocks you off of your feet! Maybe
the blow will prove to be the greatest blessing that ever came your way.

When the dark clouds of despair have darkened the pathway of life's
progress, just remember that behind each cloud is a silver lining, if
you only learn how to see it!

Two men established and built up an enormously successful
commercial institution. They owned the stock in the company about
equally. One of the men, who had lots of initiative, began selling off
some of his stock, thus enjoying for personal use a large amount of
ready cash from the proceeds.

His associate in the business, who didn't possess quite so much initiative, wanted to sell some of his personal stock that he might also enjoy some ready cash. But not a dollar could he sell. He appealed to his partner who was finding a ready market for his stock, requesting him to dispose of his stock. But the partner refused. This refusal resulted in a serious disagreement between the two men, which finally ended in a complete dissolution of their business relations.

Now let us see what happens! The one who could not find a market for his stock was the fortunate one in the final crisis. The one with the ready initiative, who sold his stock, sold with it his voice in management of the business. When the climax was reached in their disagreement, the one who couldn't sell his stock naturally had, BY FORCE OF CIRCUMSTANCES, the control of the business, so he used his power to his own salvation and to the great detriment of his associate, by voting him out of the Presidency of the corporation and voting himself into that office.

The fact that he couldn't sell his stock was A BLESSING IN DISGUISE.

A young man who was President of a corporation, which was making a great deal of money, trusted his banker too far by borrowing money for expansion purposes. The banker wanted this young man's interest in the corporation, because he knew the young man was making money and the banker happened to be dishonest. In the 1907 Roosevelt panic the banker saw his chance and closed him out. It seemed like a dark day for the young man. All was lost. But watch the roulette wheel of destiny as it spins around by the force of the hand of fate! His loss forced him to go back to the practice of law. This brought him in touch with a million-dollar corporation which employed him at a salary of $5,000 a year; a salary which he wouldn't have thought of accepting from an outsider while he was in control of his own business. This brought him to the middle west, and likewise in touch with the "big opportunity" of his life.

So his loss proved a blessing in disguise, for it literally drove him into a greater success.

A young bank clerk was discharged on account of his habit of drawing pictures and sketching mechanical parts of automobiles during business hours. The loss of his job was quite a shock to him, for he supported his mother and two sisters from his small earnings.

The loss of his bank job was the greatest blessing that ever came to him, for six months later he invented an automobile part which made him a fortune. He is now President of one of the largest automobile accessories companies in America. His clerks are all supplied with desk pads and pencils, with instructions to do all the automobile drawing they wish, and to submit to him any new ideas for improvements of automobile parts. Any of their ideas which he uses are paid for extra, at one hundred dollars each.

John D. Rockefeller discharged one of his faithful employees who he thought went too far in the exercise of his duties, in making an unauthorized financial transaction for Mr. Rockefeller in his absence, even though the deal netted Mr. Rockefeller several thousand dollars in cash.

A blessing in disguise! This man, who had been honest and faithful, but not well paid, was immediately employed by one of Mr. Rockefeller's rivals, at a handsome salary. He now holds a high official position with the rival company.

Every change in one's environment is for a purpose. That which seems like a disappointment and ill "luck" usually is a blessing in disguise. If we do not carefully study cause and effect in all that we do and all that comes our way, we may never discover when and where our apparent failures in reality are blessings.

Stop and take inventory of your own life record and see if you cannot find evidence which will support this! Take an inventory of the lives of those you know intimately and see if the same is not true!

Then, when you become discouraged; when your destiny seems doubtful, and life's pathway is fraught with many thorns of disappointment; when the rough and rugged hand of fate spins the roulette wheel of fortune so hard that the little pointer goes past your number, just remember that there is a bigger stake awaiting you, if not in your present environment, then later on, in some other "game" in the sphere of human accomplishment!

Therefore, hang on!

THE HAPPIEST MOMENT OF MY LIFE

I am going to tell you about the happiest moment I ever experienced. This little narrative will not end as you imagine it will, nor as you will believe it ought to, in all probability.

The happiest moment of my life was not the time that I secured my first position as a stenographer at $10 a week, although I was mighty happy then. To come out of the coal mines where my work was fraught with much danger, and where I had no opportunity for self-development, was indeed a happy moment. I shall never forget when I threw down my pick for the last time, feeling and knowing as I did so, that I had shaken off the shackles of drudgery which hold millions of men's noses to the grindstone of common labor for life.

Nor did I enjoy the happiest moment of my life the day I became Private Secretary to one of the greatest business executives in America, at a salary of $100 a month, even though I realized full well that this step meant the greatest opportunity that had ever come to me.

Neither did I enjoy the happiest moment of my life when I became Assistant to the Chief Counsel of one of the greatest corporations of its kind in the world. To be sure I felt the full value of this bigger opportunity for self-development, but I knew, intuitively, that I had not yet reached the happiest moment of my life.

Nor did I experience the happiest moment of my life when I became Advertising Manager for a million-dollar institution, at a salary of $5,000 a year. I felt good to see myself developing, and to know that I had progressed this far toward the goal of my final ambition, but the happiest moment of my life had not yet arrived. I realized how much further development I needed before I could begin to live and serve my fellow men in the manner that I had longed for years and years to be able to do. I saw my weakness and lack of development as no one else could have done. I knew there was still something missing, and even though I knew not what it was, I did know that without it I could never reach the height of my ambition.

I became President of a big corporation which prospered and made money. My portion of the profits were more than $1,000 a month. I had motor cars. I had servants. I had dress suits and high silk hats. I had a valet. Twelve thousand dollars a year will permit one to enjoy many things which one does not need, and without which one would be better off. BUT I WAS NOT HAPPY!

THEN CAME THE CRASH OF 1907 PANIC. In the twinkling of an eye my business and every dollar I had were swept away in that awful, though needless, panic of 1907. I went down to my office to remove the personal effects from what had been my desk the day before. In one drawer, I found a half-dollar. It was all that stood between me and starvation. I flipped the coin over in the palm of my hands a couple of times. Then came the full realization of what it was that I needed to make me happy. In those few moments, as I held that half-dollar before me, I saw myself being remelted and re-poured from the crucible of HARD EXPERIENCE!

THAT WAS THE HAPPIEST MOMENT OF MY LIFE!

I was happy because I had waded in pastures green until I had overeaten of prosperity. From a dollar a day, working as a laborer, to $1,000 a month, as President of a big corporation, was too much for me. I had to be rebaptized in the fire of want and hunger. I had to have a new foundation upon which to build my business structure. And as I sat there and took inventory of my worldly possessions, I realized full well that I would build that new and better foundation BECAUSE I HAD TO DO IT! There was no other way out, and the thought of this compulsory rebuilding process – a process which would make me stronger, more capable, and a happier worker in the harvest fields of life, brought joy to my heart.

That failure of 1907 was truly a BLESSING IN DISGUISE! Without it I would never have known the full value of adversity. It were better if we all experience temporary financial reverses. Without them we might grow selfish. We might forget that whatever worldly possessions we have we merely hold during a brief trusteeship called LIFE.

"Lord feed me not with overabundance, lest my belly become full and I deny thee."

This quotation, while it may not be exact, expresses in Biblical terms a truth which I wish to convey through this narrative. The richest experience that can come to a man or a woman is that of financial reverse. The full value of such an experience will depend upon whether we accept it as a blessing or as a curse.

Your earnest friend,

Napoleon Hill

80 East Randolph St.
Chicago, U.S.A.

GITOMER'S THOUGHTFUL ACTIONS

HOW TO IMPLEMENT THIS LESSON

Hill, by his own examples of failure, shows you how to react, respond, and recover from any situation – especially financial – AND how to turn it into a lesson rather than a defeat. Your turn. Make a list of your adversities to date, and how you reacted, responded, and recovered – next to each one, write what you COULD have done or SHOULD have done – then write the lesson learned. Interesting that what seemed devastating, at the time, now seems less of an issue. And that's a lesson all by itself. Study your past challenges and adversities – those lessons will guide you to future success.

"Every change in one's environment is for a purpose. That which seems like a disappointment and ill "luck" usually is a blessing in disguise."

– Napoleon Hill

"You can succeed in life only as you succeed in a race, by passing others."

— Napoleon Hill

Lesson Number

TIME: THE MOST PRECIOUS THING IN THE WORLD

(An after-the-lesson visit with Mr. Hill)

White Rabbit:

I'm late, I'm late for
a very important date.
No time to say hello, good-bye,
I'm late, I'm late, I'm late.

Alice's Adventures in Wonderland
– Lewis Carroll

G **GITOMER INSIGHT:** Why do the busiest people in the world ALWAYS have time to do important things? ANSWER: THEY KNOW THE VALUE OF TIME ALLOCATION AND UTILIZATION. Think of the most successful people you know. They are always busy ACHIEVING. Now think of the people you know that aren't reaching their potential. Odds are they're nowhere near maximum performance level. They blame others rather than seize opportunity. There are major answers in this lesson, but ONLY if you're willing to invest the time in yourself. More "how" answers at the end of this lesson.

James J. Hill, the great railroad builder, has passed over the Great Divide. Mr. Hill began his career as a laborer, as you know. He was not what the world would call a success until after he had passed the fortieth milepost in life. His real career began at about thirty-eight. BUT – BETWEEN THE AGES OF EIGHTEEN AND THIRTY-EIGHT HE WAS GETTING READY FOR THE SUCCESS THAT NEVER WOULD HAVE COME HAD HE NOT BEEN MAKING GOOD USE OF HIS TIME! He had his share of it and none can say that he didn't make good use of it. To him, TIME was the most important thing in the world.

By nature nearly all of us are lazy. We need constant prodding to keep us moving along in the line of self-development. Some of us are more lazy than others. These are the ones who enjoy less success – the ones which the world calls failures. Others, by constant self-development, have grown to be more industrious, and these are the ones which the world calls successful. Every one of us who is able-bodied and strong-minded, but who has failed to succeed by the time he has reached the fortieth milepost, can see the man responsible for his lack of success by looking in a looking glass.

From my office, I can look out over the beautiful blue waters of Lake Michigan. Out there in the summer, scores of young people are enjoying life in sail boats, motorboats, and canoes, just as I would like to be doing. I did pretty much as those young people are doing before I reached the age of thirty, but now TIME is too precious to be devoted entirely to pleasure. I MUST WORK FOR I AM RACING TIME AND I ONLY HAVE A FEW YEARS IN WHICH TO WIN THE RACE, UNLESS I SHOULD PROVE TO BE ONE OF THOSE WHO SUCCEED AFTER FORTY!

I am afraid, however, to take a chance on this. I have now come into possession of the most precious heritage that this world has to offer me, namely: A CHANCE TO MAKE GOOD – and I must render a good account of my stewardship. Ten years ago it would have been different. I would have said, "Oh well, what's the use of my working when I might be out having a good time," but today I cannot spare a single one of those precious hours which belong to me.

I recently read an editorial in one of our metropolitan dailies, which further impressed upon me the great value of time. That editorial was written by one of the highest-paid newspaper writers in the world, as the editorial itself forcibly indicates. It is an editorial that every man in the world, both young and old, successful and unsuccessful, ought to read. That is why I am quoting it.

It will be especially beneficial to those who have not reached the age of thirty. It will do no harm to those who have reached the age of forty or fifty. It will be beneficial to the man who wants to learn "HOW TO SELL HIS SERVICES," for it will show him "HOW TO KEEP HIS SERVICES SOLD." I shall take the liberty of giving this editorial a headline which did not appear in the paper. I shall call it – HOW TO SUCCEED!

SERMONS are tiresome and this is preaching. But a million young men, and another million would be more useful, more happy, if they could apply to themselves this sermon. It tells, in a new form, the old story of the ant and the grasshopper. La Fontaine in his fable told it to the French and to all the modern civilized world. Aesop, the Greek, of two thousand five hundred years ago, taught the story to the French writer. And to Aesop the story came from Asia. Where the Asiatic writer got it, we do not know. But we know that it is a story as old as human intelligence, but always new and true – and here it is again. And you will not waste your time if you think about it. Ant and the grasshopper meet in Cold of Winter.

The ant is comfortable, well supplied with food, for she has been working through the hot weather. The grasshopper shivering, starving, begs for help. "What have you been doing all Summer?" asked the ant. "May it please you," replied the grasshopper, "I have been singing." "Very well," says the ant, "if you have been singing all Summer, now dance in Winter." The hard-hearted ant closes the door, ends the conversation and leaves the grasshopper, who has spent the Summer singing to spend a few minutes of the Winter dying.

You young men who allow youth, which is the Summer of human beings, to drift by, working as little as you dare in Winter, working very little indeed in Summer, YOU ARE THE GRASSHOPPER OF CIVILIZATION. Later on in your Winter, in your old age, when the cold comes, and work and pay are hard to find, you will perhaps wonder at the hard-hearted selfishness of the man who has been working while you were singing, and who says, "You were singing, taking life easily, while you were young, now DANCE TO KEEP YOURSELF WARM."

The world is a great ant that has little sympathy for poverty in old age. The grasshopper of the fable was more fortunate than old men begging for work, asking for a chance that is refused, struggling vainly to make up for days wasted. Far better than cold charity and the poorhouse is the grasshopper's fate when the snow falls and frost comes.

Young men who plan their Summer vacation, and wonder how much time they will have for idleness during the warm weather, bear this in mind: YOU CAN BE ONE OF THE SUCCESSFUL MEN IF YOU WILL IT. The Successful man is one INDEPENDENT of others. The man who is not independent, lives and dies in slavery. No matter how big your pay, if you do not make yourself independent by hard work, self-control, and saving – independent of job and employer – you are nothing but your employer's slave. He owns your TIME and HE who owns your time OWNS YOU.

The man in this story is one of the human grasshoppers preparing for old age of want. He watches the bees, sees them come and go ceaselessly, all working except the one queen that produces the young bees. He knows that the drones, that do no work, are killed and thrown out of the hive by the workers at a stated time. "Interesting little creatures," says he to himself. He does not realize that he is one of the drones, waiting for old Time, the worker with his sting, to throw him out and put an end to him.

The difference between a miserable drone and worker in the hive is this: The worker has a sting, the drone has NONE. The drone is big, fat, good-looking. He will not work, and he has no sting. When the time comes, the workers attack the drones, sting them to death, drag their dead bodies out of the hive, and proceed with useful work. Young men, the sting is to the bee what WILL POWER IS TO THE MAN. Man can add to will power by CULTIVATING THE WILL, and make the will drive him to work and to independence.

Imagine a man wrecked, out in the middle of the lake, floating idly on his back, and admiring the scenery, hour after hour. You would say to him, "Young man, you had better turn over and swim toward the shore. Darkness is coming on, and you won't find your ways so easily. This is no time to be floating."

To the millions of young men, thinking only of the rest they have not earned, indulging in waste of time that means sorrow in old age, we say this: THIS IS NO TIME FOR YOU TO BE FLOATING ON YOUR BACK. This is no time for you to be admiring the scenery, wondering how you can enjoy yourself and escape unpleasant work. Winter is coming, and old age, which is the Winter of Life, is coming. Time does not stop and rest when you stop. Life is a big ocean, and you are out in the middle of it. This is the time to get toward the shore, toward safety, toward AN INDEPENDENT FOOTING.

Go to the poorhouse, to the parks where the miserable sleep at night, to the prisons, to men vainly looking for work, and you will see men who failed to swim and never reached the shore.

Now a few words for the man who is not idle, who has ambition. For him who looks upon work as the main thing, upon pleasure as secondary, the beginning of this editorial is not needed.

The time to gain success is when others stand still. He who runs while others sit and think will win the race.

The warm Summer days are days of sitting down for the majority of workers.

Everybody runs fast in the BEGINNING of a race. The cool months are the beginning of the race of each year. The hot Summer months are the end of the race. Every race is won at the END, won by the man who keeps running as fast as he can, after others have begun to get tired and go slowly.

Let you young men who have ambition be among those that run as fast in hot weather as in the days of resting, of slowing up, of sitting down.

We do not mean that you should not have reasonable vacation, if you can get it. But make it a sensible vacation. Make it all outdoor life, exercise, regular hours, careful eating, wise reading.

A vacation, reasonable in length, sane and intelligent in its use, is the most profitable part of your working year, adding years to life and efficiency to the hardworking days.

Do not, however, imagine that a reasonable vacation means a vacation free from thought.

THE BRAIN NEVER GETS TIRED.

One little part of the brain used over and over becomes fatigued. The way to rest that tired part of the brain is TO USE THE BRAIN ENERGY THAT HAS LAIN IDLE.

When you go on a vacation, you make it a point to use the muscles that have not been working. Make it also a point to use these parts of the brain that have not been working.

"A vacation, reasonable in length, sane and intelligent in its use, is the most profitable part of your working year, adding years to life and efficiency to the hardworking days."

– Napoleon Hill

Read good books, a new kind. Think earnestly on new subjects. Question those with whom you come in contact. Find out how THEY live – the real study of mankind is man, as you know. Study yourself, while you are working, to make sure that you are doing your best. Study others on your vacation, talk with them, question them, LISTEN to them, that you may learn from others, and from the thoughts of others.

When Darwin went on his famous ocean trip, he might have made it a vacation in the usual sense. It was a vacation, but it made him a greater man in science, better, more useful. He brought back knowledge and health from his vacation. See that you do the same.

Ambitious young men, you should realize that days of idleness for others are YOUR OPPORTUNITY.

You can succeed in life only as you succeed in a race, by passing others. And you can succeed most easily while the other man is sleeping in the hammock, drowsing, "floating" on his back getting nowhere, not realizing that he is far from the shore of independence.

HE REPRESENTS YOUR OPPORTUNITY.

For this is a world of competition, and success is built on the failure of others. An intelligent young man said to his father there were too many fools in the world. "Don't be too hard on fools," said the father. "If there were not so many fools, we might not be so well off."

Very cordially yours,

Napoleon Hill

80 East Randolph St.
Chicago, U.S.A.

GITOMER'S THOUGHTFUL ACTIONS

HOW TO IMPLEMENT THIS LESSON

"Time is money." You've heard that expression a thousand times
or more. And as many times as you've heard it, *you have universally
ignored it.* So if time is money, what are you doing with yours? Are
you spending it or investing it? And how are your time investments
working for you? Hill stresses the value of time and gives examples of
how to utilize it for maximum return. Here's what to do:

1. Identify your 4–5 most important uses of time. Family,
exercise, sales career, travel, whatever.

2. Create a WEEKLY TIME ALLOCATION chart. Divide your daily
awake time into 30-minute segments.

**3. Enter the IMPORTANT elements from #1 into the chart
as necessary.** This will allow you to concentrate on the
IMPORTANT elements of your life.

"Do not, however, imagine that a reasonable vacation means a vacation free from thought.

THE BRAIN NEVER GETS TIRED."

– Napoleon Hill

Lesson Number

SEVEN SUCCESS RULES

(An after-the-lesson visit with Mr. Hill)

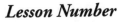 **GITOMER INSIGHT: Everyone is looking for the secrets to success. If this is you, STOP LOOKING and start reading and studying. There is no "one" secret. But there are ideas, strategies, thoughts, and philosophies that you can adapt and adopt to your personal situation, desires, family needs, and work ethic. Here are Hill's rules. And once you read them, you will see that they are ALL immediately adaptable AND adoptable into your life.**

Well, here we are, on the ninth lesson! You have now passed over the dryest part of your course. From now on you will be walking in clover up to your eyes. The work will be so intensely interesting that you will look forward to the receipt of your lesson assignments with as much eagerness as a boy who expected a new glove, ball, and bat.

We have many surprises in store for you!

We are going to give you much more than we promised when you began this course. You have been faithful thus far. You have gone over the dull portion of the course in a way that proves that you have will power, determination, and stick-to-it-iveness. You have shown faith, not only in your instructors BUT IN YOURSELF AS WELL! Congratulations! The man who believes in himself has his battle for SUCCESS nine parts won.

In this little visit with you, I am going to give you what I believe to be seven of the most important rules for success – rules which all men who have succeeded have observed in some form or other. Mind you, I do not say that even strict observance of these rules alone will make you successful, but it will go a long way toward it. The first rule is one that I am perfectly sure you ought to observe. Some of these rules I lay claims to, while others were suggested by an editorial which appeared in one of the great Metropolitan newspapers; just which one I do not now recall – if I did I would gladly give credit. Here are the rules:

FIRST: You must believe in yourself. You must cultivate SELF-CONFIDENCE!

I place this above all the others because I believe it to be the most important. Many years ago, three young men graduated from Business College and went out into the world to build their careers. Two of them had only common school educations while the third was a college graduate. One of the "common-school" boys is now Advertising Manager of one of New York's largest Department Stores at a salary of $10,000 a year. The other "common-school" boy is writing this little "after-the-lesson visit" for you. And the college graduate – well, his record is not what we two "ordinary" boys thought it would be.

He came in to see me a few months ago. He had on a dirty shirt. His shoes were out at the toes. He was the worst-looking "tramp" I had seen in a long while. I hadn't seen him for ten years, so I didn't know him at first.

He told me his story. He had failed in everything he undertook. I took him home with me, gave him a suit of clothes, a clean shirt and collar, and got him a job. The next day he was back again. He had lost his job! The trouble was lack of SELF-CONFIDENCE. Nothing else under the sun! He had schooling a plenty. He had plenty of common sense. But what he didn't have was faith in himself, so he is a miserable failure.

SECOND: You must cultivate ENTHUSIASM.

ENTHUSIASM is one of the great factors in success. It is important especially because IT HELPS A MAN GET A START.

Unfortunately, enthusiasm is one of the qualities most difficult to cultivate. It is almost a part of a man's own self, like his dark hair, wide shoulders, or regular features. Yet even enthusiasm CAN be cultivated, and it should be cultivated.

Begin by getting out of your mind the critical, complaining, dissatisfied feelings. That is like pulling weeds out of a field. If a man can get out of his mind the foolish feeling of complaint, of mortified vanity, he will be clearing the field for enthusiasm to grow.

Enthusiasm is largely a matter of vitality, health, and strength. Get up in the morning after eight hours good sleep, and you will be enthusiastic – ready to attack any proposition. Get up with five hours' sleep and a night foolishly spent, and you will have no strength for enthusiasm. Cultivate your strength, save it, and train yourself to look enthusiastically, and hopefully at the world, and scorn its difficulties! Enthusiasm is the electric power which runs the motor of self-confidence!

THIRD: It is unnecessary to suggest that you must be honest. Honesty has been talked of incessantly ever since the writing of the Ten Commandments, and long before. There are many false reputations and not a few big fortunes built on DISHONESTY. There are some men poor now who might have been rich if they had been dishonest. But be sure that REAL success comes only to the honest man who thinks and works and TREATS OTHER MEN HONESTLY.

FOURTH: You must practice Self-Denial.

SELF-DENIAL is especially a matter of self-education.

Instead of putting your mind on the question, "How can I amuse myself or dress myself?" say to yourself, "What can I DO

WITHOUT?" Self-denial is not important simply because it saves your money – it is especially important because IT SAVES YOUR TIME AND YOUR VITALITY.

Sobriety is, of course, a part of self-denial. If you don't smoke excessively, if you don't drink excessively – you save money and you save vitality. If you don't pay foolish attention to dress – only neatness and common sense are necessary to success – you save the time and the thought that many men put on worthless worrying about their personal appearance.

The most important in the line of self-denial, perhaps, is TO MAKE YOURSELF NOT WORRY ABOUT WHAT OTHERS THINK OF YOU. Try to earn the approval of those who are worthwhile, and dismiss from your mind the opinion of the crowd that means nothing to you and can do nothing for you. More men waste time and energy and worry on the opinion of others – more than enough to make them successful if they would be indifferent to worthless public opinion.

FIFTH: You must use your own will power.

What you do MUST BE DONE ABSOLUTELY BY THE EXERCISE OF YOUR OWN WILL POWER. IF YOU DECEIVE YOURSELF, AND BLAME OTHERS INSTEAD OF YOURSELF, YOU WILL NEVER GET AHEAD. YOU MUST BE YOUR OWN MOST SEVERE JUDGE. Remember that it is not sufficient to WISH for success or to ADMIRE the qualities that make success; you must develop those qualities, and use them.

SIXTH: You must be unselfish, if you would have Dame Fortune smile upon you.

Unselfishness is the greatest, highest quality of all. Any man who would be truly great in his achievements must have for his inspiration an unselfish desire to be of use to other men. He may pile up millions, but he will not be one of the world's really great men unless guided by the consciousness that a man's first and last duty is to try to make others better off and happier for his having lived on the earth.

SEVENTH: You must concentrate in all your efforts – in all your work.

The necessity of concentration can never be too much insisted upon. All kinds of success in the world depend upon it. Young people who think that genius or luck will carry them through make a terrible mistake. Genius and what is called luck ARE concentration and nothing else.

What concentration means may be illustrated by examples. When Abraham Lincoln was a boy, he used to listen to the talk of his elders. Out in that new country where he lived, everybody talked politics.

Young Abraham did not know much about politics then, but he knew that the men who did know got ahead in the world somehow, and he determined to understand such things for himself.

Accordingly, he listened intently every time he heard a political discussion. At first he understood very little, but he only listened harder and thought over what he had heard. After a while he began to understand. Then he put his mind so closely to work upon the subjects discussed by the debaters that he was able not only to see what they were driving at, but to improve their methods of explaining their thoughts.

He saw that a large part of the difficulty that he had experienced in following them arose from the fact that they neither saw clearly what they wished to say, nor expressed it in clear language. He got hold of the general idea of a speaker and went on by himself and labored over it in his own mind, putting it in more expressive words, and reshaping it in a more logical form, until it became as clear as crystal. Finally, he surprised his elders by stating their ideas better than they could state them themselves.

Now, THAT WAS CONCENTRATION, and Lincoln practiced it until it became the settled habit of his mind. It made him President of the United States and the clear-headed leader of his country in the most threatening crisis that ever passed.

There was once a little boy in the city of Utrecht, the son of a poor workingman, who was determined to get an education. He showed so much earnestness in his ambition that he attracted the attention of good people who obtained his admittance as a free scholar in the University of Louvain. While the scholars who could pay did what was required of them in a half-hearted way and spent as much time as possible in idle amusements, he was not content with the lessons of the day, but borrowed books to study at night. Because he was too poor to have candles, he spent a part of each night studying his books by the light of street lamps or in illuminated church porches. That, too, was CONCENTRATION, and the young scholar carried it so far that he was made preceptor to the man who was to be the great Emperor Charles V.

When James Ferguson was seven or eight years old, the roof of his father's cottage in Scotland fell in, and he saw his father take a beam to pry up the fallen roof. The boy was astonished because the beam seemed to give his father the strength of a giant. He watched how it was used, then experimented with sticks, and discovered, unaided, the mechanical principle of the lever.

But observing that the long end of a lever had to be moved through an inconveniently great distance in order to produce a slight movement of the weight to be raised, he reasoned upon the matter so closely that he invented a wheel and axle to do more easily the work of a long lever. Thus, by simple concentration of mind, this boy discovered for himself a great mechanical truth, which, as he did not then know, had occupied the inventive powers of famous men for centuries.

The habit of mental concentration which he established at so early an age made him afterward one of the most celebrated and influential men of his time.

These are concrete examples of concentration. They could be multiplied a thousandfold, but let us glance at the principle that underlies them. That principle is simply CLOSE UNDIVIDED ATTENTION. The thing that makes men failures is dissipation of the mind. Don't let your attention wander; hold your mind firmly upon the subject before it! Stick to it until you have got to the bottom of it. Avoid darting from one thing to another, leaving each half finished! If you are learning to pitch a baseball, you keep at it until, gradually, your hand and arm appear to have acquired magical power over the ball. You can do the same thing with your mind; you can make it so effective by concentration that you will be able to control events and turn them to advantage.

But you have to make a start! You have to try! Success only comes to those who look for it – those who try! Success never collided with a procrastinator – the man who says, "I'll think it over until tomorrow." Tomorrow never comes! So make use of today while your light is yet shining.

I want you to be guided by my recommendations and purchase a copy of a little book, by Dr. F. W. Sears, entitled *CONCENTRATION*. It will cost you only a half-dollar and you can probably get it at any bookstore. If not, send a half-dollar direct to the Institute, and they will purchase a copy and send it to you. This little book can be read in less than an hour. It will give you a better understanding of Concentration than you ever had before. It will show you exactly how to concentrate! I have read it many times as has Mrs. Hill. We find something new every time we read it.

I also recommend that you purchase a copy of *As a Man Thinketh*, by James Allen. This will give you an understanding of the mind power which you possess, from a new viewpoint, unless you have read the book already. You can get it at any bookstore for a quarter. I have read this book more than a dozen times. It is of great practical value to a student of Life and Success and Salesmanship.

⬛ GITOMER NOTE: Both books can be found at HillsFirstWritings.com.

From time to time, as you go along with your course, I will recommend to you good, helpful books. I will recommend no book that will not be of practical value to you as a student of Success and Salesmanship. Furthermore, I will recommend only books that are within your means. Every student of Success and Salesmanship ought to keep well informed through the numerous magazines and books on the subject of Success and Selling. For ten dollars a year or less you may have the pick of the best publications available on the subject of Success and Salesmanship. To read these magazines and analyze them carefully is a splendid education within itself. They will keep your mind directed in the field in which you are interested, and you will pick up many a good practical idea that will serve you well in the years to come.

Yours for a successful career,

Napoleon Hill

Napoleon Hill

G GITOMER'S THOUGHTFUL ACTIONS

HOW TO IMPLEMENT THIS LESSON

Since the Bible and the 10 Commandments, everyone has been given their rules for success or ideas about how to succeed better. This is a set of rules about how YOU can get better. These rules apply to everyday life as well as years in your future. This is a lesson to read, study, memorize, and practice EVERY DAY.

List the seven rules and rate yourself from 1-10 on your present success level. Between your rating and 10 lies your GAP. Taking daily steps toward improving EACH ONE will ultimately get you closer to the goal – but the secret to actually taking these steps is in the previous lesson: ALLOCATE TIME. Make appointments with yourself to create success time.

10

ADOPT A "CHIEF AIM IN LIFE"!

(An after-the-lesson visit with Mr. Hill)

G **GITOMER INSIGHT: Keep in mind that this lesson and philosophy were written 20 years BEFORE *Think and Grow Rich*. And this is the first writing where "Chief Aim" is defined. Hill was perfecting this success and wealth-building strategy at the very outset of his own career. There's a free booklet offered in this lesson that reveals Hill's source for this concept. It's as fascinating as it is accurate.**

Among the thousand and one little things which go to make up the qualifications necessary in the thoroughly efficient man is the all-important faculty of working with a definite purpose in view – with a "chief aim in life."

I was reminded of this very forcibly one summer at a bathing beach here in Chicago. It was Sunday, and I was taking a little outing with my wife and two boys; I was strolling along, watching the bathers in the surf and the happy children playing in the sand. Not far from me a boy was playing with a large shepherd dog; a little farther down on the beach was a family consisting of a father, mother, and child. The child had a little half-grown fox terrier puppy; and as I looked on, the antics of the two dogs reminded me of life and men.

The boy with the shepherd dog would throw a stick out into the breakers and tell the dog to go after it, and the noble fellow would look up into his master's face, and one could almost fancy that he said, "You watch me, I'll get the stick," and he did get it every time.

He would plunge into the surf and fight his way out to it and bring it back to shore, and after laying it at his master's feet would look up into his face with an expression that seemed to say, "There, I did it, didn't I?" He had accomplished something; he knew it and was pleased, no matter that time and time again the breakers carried him almost back to shore. He had made up his mind that he would get that stick, and he got it.

Now, all this time, what was the little fox terrier doing? Was he watching the older and wiser dog and profiting by his example? No, not he! He was digging a hole in the sand! What for? Oh, just to be digging! Perhaps there were rats or gophers in the sand and he was after them? No, that was not it, and, besides, he wouldn't know a gopher from a sand crab; he was just digging a hole in the sand. Just wasting his energy and accomplishing nothing, and all the time he was making a great fuss over it.

He would dig a while, and bark a while, and dig a while, and bark a while, and the mere fact that no one seemed to notice him didn't seem to bother him in the least. He just kept on digging and barking, and all the time the shepherd dog continued to go after the stick and get it every time.

He was digging, too, but with a definite purpose in view, and he wasn't making a sound; and each successive time he came in with the stick, he received a little fonder pat on the head, which assured him that his efforts were appreciated. He was making good, and, oh, the satisfaction of it! And then he barked, and his bark seemed to say to the boy, "Throw it out again, I'll bring it back; the breakers are never too high for me."

And – well, I declare, we almost forgot the puppy dog. What was he getting for his labor? Most of the time they did not pay any attention to him at all, but once in a while they noticed him long enough to give him a cuff on the ear and say, "Quit that you little fool, you're scratching sand all over the lunch," but he kept on digging the hole in the sand, and finally it was so deep that we couldn't see him at all.

He had been digging so long and so persistently that he had disappeared from our vision, and if he had not continued to make such infernal noise with his barking, we would have forgotten that he was in the land of the living.

Do you see anything in this, I wonder?

Figuratively speaking, what are You? Are you a shepherd or a fox terrier? Do you work with a purpose in view? Or are you digging a hole in the sand and barking all the time you are digging it? If you are, look out! You may dig it so deep that you can never climb out of it, and the walls, being sand, may crumble and fall on you, and you will find yourself buried under the foolish mistakes of the past, while your friend, the shepherd dog, will have graduated from the stick-chasing stage because he has demonstrated that he always gets it when he goes after it, and he can be depended upon to do things.

And so it goes. We go from day to day, year to year, accusing opportunity of playing favorites because she doesn't knock at our door. All the time she is standing before us, just begging us to embrace her. She stands up by our couch when we sleep, and she cries out in a loud voice, "WAKE UP! I'M HERE!" But we sleep on, and when we are told that she was there and that she tried with all her might to wake us, we rub our eyes and say, "Oh, well, she didn't try very hard, I guess; why didn't she shake me?" And we go out and dig a little more in the sand.

But don't lose heart! She is still there, standing right outside of your door now, and all that is necessary is for you to call her and convince her that you want her, and she'll come in and prove that at least one old adage is a joke, and that is that "Opportunity never knocks but once."

Cover up the hole you have been digging. Stop your barking. Get your eyes on the stick as it floats out on the breakers of life. Go after it. And don't come back until you get it! If the breakers knock you down time and time again, spit out the water, shake your head and go after it; and when you get back to shore, you'll be more than glad you did it.

Never mind the hole you were so long in digging; just go back and look for it, and you'll find that it has disappeared. That charitable waves of life smoothed it all down at high tide; they will always do that when they see that you are through with it. Turn your back on it! Hold out your arm to Opportunity, and as you stroll down life's sands, with her at your side, keep your eye on the breakers as they roll in from the mighty ocean and LOOK OUT FOR MORE STICKS! When you see them, GO AFTER THEM.

You will be better prepared to go after the sticks after you read the little booklet that you will receive with this lesson, entitled "The Law of Financial Success." (Go to HillsFirstWritings.com and get your free copy.)

But before you start on the booklet, draw up your chairs and let me tell you how it came to be a part of your lesson in life. One Sunday morning I was on my way to my home to write this "visit." Across the aisle from me in the streetcar, sat an old man who was fumbling with a little brown-covered booklet. A strange feeling of curiosity to see the booklet came over me, so I walked over and sat down beside him and looked over his shoulder until I caught the name of the publisher. Next day, I requested my Secretary to write for a copy, which came in due time.

As I began to read it, I saw an unusual resemblance between my own philosophy and that of the writer of the booklet, to say nothing of the resemblance in our style of writing. I turned back hurriedly to see the date of the copyright, believing that someone had "cribbed" some of my work, when lo! I discovered that the booklet had been written nearly ten years previously.

I never saw the booklet until then, and had never even heard of it. Just why I was so strongly drawn to it, even before I saw the title is a bit of strange phenomena which I shall not undertake to explain. I have tried out every one of the principles which it champions, in the great workshop of life, and can heartily endorse them as being sound and practical. Through the operation of these principles you can acquire not only money, but any material thing that exists in this world.

The booklet is presented to you at this time for the reason that we will be making application of the principles which it sets forth throughout your course. Do not stop by reading the booklet once. Read it twice, three times – even a dozen times. Mark the points which you can corroborate with your own experience. It will give you a wonderful grip on the philosophy of life generally.

Earnestly yours for a great understanding
of the powers that are within your mind,

Napoleon Hill

Napoleon Hill

Ⓖ GITOMER'S THOUGHTFUL ACTIONS

HOW TO IMPLEMENT THIS LESSON

This is the turning point of the book. This is where you focus and dedicate or rededicate yourself to a life of personal excellence with a definite major aim and purpose. Take the time to write yours down. Start your focus every morning. Stay on the path until you have grown past it. That's correct, you will achieve and grow to "what's next?" But the same rule applies. Create the aim and the purpose, and with dedication and desire, all is possible.

"Big pay and little responsibility are circumstances seldom found together."

— *Napoleon Hill*

Lesson Number

11

THE "LAW OF HARMONIOUS ATTRACTION"

(An after-the-lesson visit with Mr. Hill)

G GITOMER INSIGHT: It's amazing how ahead of his time Napoleon Hill really was. "The Law of Attraction" has been bantered around for more than a century, but here Hill, with one simple adjective, makes the reader understand that simply saying, "The Law of Attraction" does not bring clarity to the law. Add "harmonious" to the law and it becomes both understandable AND actionable.

One of the best lessons on Salesmanship that I ever learned was drawn from my experience with the Chicago Press Club, as related to "The Psychology of Salesmanship."

The next best lesson in Salesmanship that I ever learned was drawn from an experience with my two small boys. Every Sunday morning we are in the habit of walking across the park to the lakefront for a little visit. The boys always stop at the peanut stand on the corner and take along some nuts for the squirrels in the park. On this particular Sunday morning "Nap, Junior" got a bag of peanuts and "Jimmy" purchased a box of popcorn called "Crispettes."

As we walked along through the park, Jimmy reached over and made a grab for the bag of peanuts which Nap was carrying. He missed the bag, and by way of retaliation Nap struck at him and said, "Let 'em alone!"

Then I said to Jimmy, "Now let me show you how to get some of those peanuts. You open up your box of Crispettes and offer some to Nap and see what happens." Jimmy did as I told him, but before Nap would accept any of the popcorn, he insisted on opening up the bag of peanuts and pouring some of them into Jimmy's pocket.

Now this may seem to you to be a very simple illustration of the Psychology of Salesmanship, and it is! However, I wish to leave this thought with you – most of us are just children, like Nap and Jimmy when it comes to returning favors. If I do you a favor, it makes no difference how slight, you will be pretty apt to reciprocate. You may take the meanest and most unpolished man of your acquaintance, give him a good reputation and let him know that you are willing to help him, and he will do everything in his power to live up to that reputation in nine cases out of ten.

The world is a great big looking glass in which we reflect that which is in our own hearts and minds!

I will admit that sometimes that glass becomes blurred and apparently it does not reflect the true image before it. However, you can wipe off the blur, polish the surface of the glass, and behold! You will see exactly what the world sees in you. If you will radiate hope, sunshine, good cheer, and optimism, you will be sure to see those same qualities in those around you.

There is nothing new or revealing about this. It is according to well-established and generally accepted laws of both physiology and psychology.

"AS A MAN THINKETH IN HIS HEART, SO IS HE."

This quotation is more than an axiom – it is a scientific truth that you and I can and should make use of. The facts are that WE ARE MAKING USE OF IT whether we realize it or not. We are either consciously or unconsciously creating a material condition in life that is an exact reproduction of that which we are creating in thought!

Tell me, if you can, of any material thing that man ever created in the physical world, of any house he ever built, of any automobile he ever invented, of any machinery he ever constructed, that was not first created in THOUGHT in his or in another's mind!

Go back and again read that little booklet, "The Law of Financial Success," **(HillsFirstWritings.com)** that came with your last lesson. In it you will find all of the philosophy that you will need with which to ATTRACT TO YOU anything that you DESIRE! The DESIRE that you hold uppermost in your mind may be likened to CAUSE while the object of that desire may be likened to EFFECT. Remember, then, that if the *effect* is not satisfactory, you should reshape the *cause*.

I have told this little story concerning my two boys as a simple illustration of a great and powerful principle that will aid you in everything you do if you will understand and apply it. In writing collection letters, you can especially make use of this principle, because most people respond readily to friendly suggestion whereas they rebel violently at force or threats of any nature.

Yes, it will help you over many a tough spot if you remember that little "peanut and popcorn" story of the Hill Juniors. Watch the person who comes to you laden with gifts and seeking the opportunity to please you, for such a person is a master salesman and may prove to be your match. Without even attempting to understand the reason why, you will agree that it is better to please than to antagonize the person of whom you intend to ask favors. You will just as readily agree that the best way to gain the cooperation of others is by first having cooperated with them or indicated your willingness to do so.

If you want favors bestow favors!

If you want trouble, "start something" and you'll find it! This is in accordance with the "Law of Harmonious Attraction" through the operation of which we *get* exactly what we *give*!

The human race is selfish! We favor others because they have favored us. We speak well of others because they have spoken well of us, but just let us hear of an uncomplimentary remark that someone, whom we had until then held in the highest of esteem, makes about us, and instantly our opinion concerning that person changes.

It is not only a sure indication of your bigness, but a mighty good sign that you are a diplomat and a salesman when you indicate a willingness to forgive the man who has been unkind toward you. The greatest punishment you can mete out to a person who had done you an injury is to meet him with a smile and a glad handshake at the first opportunity. You can change a lifelong foe into a warm and loyal friend in ten seconds if you will first eliminate from your heart all feelings of hatred and revenge and then make that foe feel that you think well of him. I know this can be done for I have tried it, not only once but on several occasions.

The surest way to defeat your adversary who approaches you in a spirit of anger is to reply in a calm tone, and in a spirit of friendliness.

I do not know why it is, but I DO KNOW THAT IT IS – that all obstacles in life's pathway vanish instantly before the person who can FORGIVE AND FORGET – the person who can love instead of hate!

If you have not learned to really see the good there is in everyone, even the person who has unjustly offended you and imposed upon you, you have overlooked the greatest of all powers for success. Learn to love the person who has wronged you, if for no other reason than the fact that this will give you strength and power that will place you head and shoulders above that person.

If you strike back in thought and in deed every time a person wrongs you, that person is lowering you to his level. He is bringing you down to his plane. He is dominating you. His will power is the stronger of the two. On the other hand, if you refuse to pollute your mind and discolor the beauty of your soul just because someone else has done so, you possess infinitely greater wisdom than the other person, and, in turn, you will wield infinitely greater power than he could.

To control others, you must first learn to control yourself!

One of the curses of humanity is the lack of self-control – the disposition to strike back every time some other person gives us cause for offense. But for Intolerance the world would be a thousand years ahead of our present state of civilization!

Take those chips off your shoulders! They have no place in this twentieth-century civilization. They belong to the stone age. Uncontrolled tempers have stood between millions of men and a higher and bigger success.

"Whom the gods would destroy they first make mad."

I do not recall whose philosophy this is, but I DO KNOW that it is sound.

Of course, you ought to know the truth of these principles as well as I do, but if perchance you should doubt them, in part or in whole, just try them out. Go to the person who has been in the habit of passing you by with his nose tilted in the air at a forty-five-degree angle, step in front of him, hold out your hand, and make him shake it! Let him see by the sparkle in your eyes and the grip of your hand that you mean it. The chances are that his under jaw will drop, his mouth will fall open, and he will stare at you in amazement. He will clearly see that you are a bigger man than he is, and in the secret depths of his heart he will want to emulate you.

AND THE VERY NEXT TIME HE MEETS YOU, HE WILL!

"If you want favors bestow favors!…This is in accordance with the 'Law of Harmonious Attraction' through the operation of which we *get* exactly what we *give*!"

— *Napoleon Hill*

He will not let you "outdo" him in politeness. He may not reason the matter out in just this way, but that is what will take place in his mind whether he is conscious of it or not.

I tell you, my friends, you are creating your own atmosphere wherever you go. You are making people admire you – you are making them want to serve you and do your bidding, or you are causing them to dislike you and to shrink away from you. Whichever it is, you are the person responsible for it.

Make your thoughts right and your acts will be in harmony with your thoughts. If your outward acts are right, they will attract people to you.

Suppose that you are an employee and you feel that your employer has been unkind to you and unappreciative of your services! Man alive! Can you not see that you have the whip in your own hands and that you make him cringe in the dust at your bidding?

HOW?

Now I ask you to answer that for yourself. Think it out and then try it. As a mere suggestion for a beginning, suppose that you start in and for a few days do more work and better work than you have been in the habit of doing. If you are supposed to get to work at 8:30 and leave at 5:30, change your hours during this experiment and get there at eight and leave at six. Do, not only the things that you are supposed to do, but go out of your way to do the things that you are not supposed to do. Go to your employer when you have a few minutes of spare time and ask permission to take on a few additional responsibilities. Of course, I will admit that he will stop and look at you in amazement, and possibly he will ask you to repeat to make sure that he understood you, but you do this and then make good on whatever additional work he gives you to perform.

Proceed along this line for a week or so. If you have been in the habit of speaking slightingly of your employer, change your attitude, and during this experiment speak of him in the highest of terms. Speak of him often. Let him know that you are speaking of him in this complimentary manner. Let your fellow workers know it. If you will make an honest experiment such as this, you will see a miracle before long. Your employer will begin to show partiality toward you. He will go out of his way to say a kind word to you.

If you will keep up this "experiment" long enough, you will soon learn something concerning the "Law of Harmonious Attraction." Furthermore, you will be on the road to a bigger position or to a partnership in the business. If not with your present employer, then with some other employer who will have heard of your "strange" action. Yes, strange – so strange that it seldom happens. You will have but little competition in this experiment. But a few have tried it – just a few men such as Carnegie, Hill, Rockefeller, Schwab, Vanderlip, Harriman, Edward Bok, and a few others of their type.

"WHATSOEVER YE SOWETH THAT SHALL YE ALSO REAP."

It is as true today as it was two thousand years ago. It will work just as well now as it did then.

Cordially and sincerely your friend,

Napoleon Hill

Napoleon Hill
80 East Randolph St.
Chicago, U.S.A.

G GITOMER'S THOUGHTFUL ACTIONS

HOW TO IMPLEMENT THIS LESSON

Harmonious Attraction means finding people that match your philosophy, match your ethics, have a service heart, and have long-term relationship potential. It redefines what you have come to know as "The Law of Attraction" – this is by far the easiest of lessons to implement – your actions will attract the best, if you are the best.

> "We are either consciously or unconsciously creating a material condition in life that is an exact reproduction of that which we are creating in thought!"
>
> – Napoleon Hill

"Ambition is the great weapon with which you must fight your way to the top."

– *Napoleon Hill*

Lesson Number

12

HOW TO SELL YOURSELF AND YOUR SERVICES

(An after-the-lesson visit with Mr. Hill)

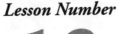 **GITOMER INSIGHT: This is about making the ultimate sale, selling yourself. The first sale that's made is the salesperson. If the customer, or the prospect, or the banker doesn't buy you, nothing else you say matters. Here is Hill's personal guide, based on his incredible communication, persuasion, and selling skills. Note the insight into human nature and how significant a role it plays.**

I suppose that nothing is of more interest to all of us than knowledge of HOW TO SELL OUR SERVICES for more money. First of all, to get more we must give more. In some instances we must give greater quantity. In other instances we must give better quality. In still other instances we must give both greater quantity and better quality of service.

As a general rule we do not get more for our services than the price we place upon them. No merchant ever sold a suit of clothes for $30 which was only marked $25. No man ever became a $1,800-a-year man who set his own price at only $1,200.

"If you are not in a line of business that will stand a higher price for the kind of work you are performing, you know the remedy. Get out and get into some other business."

– Napoleon Hill

I began as a laborer at a dollar a day. Through the efforts of a man who gave me courage, inspiration, and self-confidence, I became a stenographer and went to work at $10 a week. Pretty soon ambition began to call and I boosted my price to $50 a month. I didn't get it right away but eventually I did. Mind you, however, I didn't get $55 – just $50 – the price I had set. Ambition began to prod me a little more, so I boosted my price tag to $75 a month. Very soon I was getting $75 – but not $80 or $90. Then I raised the price again to $100 a month, and soon I was getting exactly that amount, but no more.

Then I began to gain self-confidence pretty rapidly, so I next boosted my price to $150 a month, and soon I was getting that amount, but not any more. The next time I boosted the price to $2,000 a year and got it. Then to $2,500, and soon I was getting exactly this sum. Right along there was where I began to "find myself." I next boosted my price tag to $5,000 a year, and within six months after I made up my mind to raise the price, I was getting just this sum.

But there is a point I would not have you miss – FROM THE VERY MOMENT THAT I RAISED MY PRICE TAG TO A HIGHER FIGURE, I COMMENCED TO BELIEVE I WAS WORTH MORE, AND TO DO MY LEVEL BEST TO BE ACTUALLY WORTH MORE! My every thought and action had a tendency toward making me more efficient every time I would raise my price.

> **G GITOMER NOTE: $150,000 piece of advice:** In January of 1996, I had just raised my fee from $5,000 per speech to $6,000. On coincidence I ran into the *Business Journal* publisher and friend Mark Ethridge in the Charlotte airport. He was the first to publish my column in the paper (1992) and exposed me to the world of sales and business. We were both flying to Dallas. And we were sitting together! Coincidence? I don't believe in them. "What's your speaking fee this year?" he asked. "I just raised it to six thousand," I said with pride. "What was it last year?" he asked. "Five thousand,"

> I said. "Are you 20 percent better this year?" he
> asked. "Uh, I, ah, don't know," I stammered. "Your
> fee is in your head," he said matter-of-factly. That
> was January 10. I came home from Dallas and
> immediately raised my fee to $7,500. I gave 100
> speeches that year and made an EXTRA $150K
> based on "internal belief." Hill is on the money
> here – make it your money. I did.

When an employee commences to render better service, as a rule he
or she very soon attracts the attention of those who have authority to
increase salaries.

In the new book which I have just completed, entitled *HOW TO
SELL YOUR SERVICES*, Mr. Andrew Carnegie reminds us, an
article which he wrote on this subject, that to merely render good
services is not enough – that we must ATTRACT ATTENTION of
our superiors. Personally, I believe that a mighty good way to attract
attention is to render services that are just a little better in quality and
greater in amount than we are actually being paid to render.

But I will agree that this is not always sufficient. Some employers
have very poor eyesight when it comes to seeing an employee's efforts
to render more and better service. Sometimes such employers must
be reminded of their duty. In other instances we have to look for
employers whose eyesight is better.

My plan has always been to render service which satisfied me that
it was worth more money, before asking for it. If you cannot give a
good reason why you should have an increase, do not ask for it. Place
yourself in the employer's position. Ask yourself what YOU would do
if your employer were you and you were he. This test usually gives us
a pretty accurate estimate of our own worth.

Many of us are engaged in work, the very nature of which does not
permit a greater remuneration. In such cases the only thing to do is
to enter a bigger field, where opportunity is broader. Look ahead one,
two, three, or five years and see just what there is in the position you

now hold, on the hypothesis that you will render service that is right in both QUALITY and QUANTITY. If you do not see a clear track, it may be well for you to select another field now. Do not permit yourself to become self-satisfied. Ambition is the great weapon with which you must fight your way to the top. Mark up your price tag. If you are not in a line of business that will stand a higher price for the kind of work you are performing, you know the remedy. Get out and get into some other business.

Very cordially your friend,

Napoleon Hill

Napoleon Hill
80 East Randolph Street
Chicago, U.S.A.

🅖 GITOMER'S THOUGHTFUL ACTIONS

HOW TO IMPLEMENT THIS LESSON

What VALUE do you bring to others? What wisdom are you providing without expectation of return? What are you worth as a person? Is that the rate at which you're earning? Maybe you're not giving value or service better than you're paid to deliver. Would you pay your rate? How can you increase your personal value you offer to your employer? Hill says time and time again to render more service than is expected of you. Are you doing more than expected? Or are you still sporting the loser's philosophy of "They don't pay me enough…" Winner or whiner? The choice is obvious to me. You? Service comes from your heart – not from your head. Service is not a policy, it's a PERSON! Be that person and you will win in sales and in life.

"The road that leads to happiness has its beginning so close to where you are this very moment that you may not see it. The beginning is in your heart and brain, where you may lay hold of it if you will!"

— *Napoleon Hill*

Lesson Number

13

DISCOVERY; THINGS, LIFE, and HAPPINESS

(An after-the-lesson visit with Mr. Hill)

 **GITOMER INSIGHT: Self-discovery is the underlying theme of this lesson. Hill reveals the wonder of "finding yourself" and the elements (good and bad) of what makes it happen. The revelations inside this lesson are both life enhancing and life changing, but only if you're willing to take a close look at yourself.**

The sun disappears beyond the western horizon. We press a button and create its counterpart because Edison discovered the incandescent electric light.

An operator touches a key, and with a few movements of the hand he flashes a message to a ship in mid-ocean, or to a receiving station on the other side of the earth – because Marconi discovered wireless telegraphy.

A young woman rises to a height of several thousand feet in the air, and within a few hours time she flies from Chicago to New York, a thousand miles, because the Wright brothers discovered the aeroplane.

"Picture in your mind the objective – the final goal you are striving to reach.

Then, through the power of strong desire, concentrate all your efforts on that objective until you reach it."

– *Napoleon Hill*

Through the discovery of the submarine we may sit comfortably upon the bottom of the ocean and watch the queer monsters of the sea.

Through the discovery of the X-Ray we may take a photograph of the interior of the human body.

Through the discovery of the automobile we can speed over the ground at the rate of a hundred miles an hour.

All these wonderful things have been discovered during the 20th Century. They were here all the time, but we hadn't discovered them yet.

But these remarkable mechanical discoveries are by no means the greatest discovery of the 20th Century. We have made one other discovery, which far surpasses all these.

We have discovered how to be happy!

This discovery was made by a little, old woman whose lease on life had almost expired. Her name was Mary Baker Eddy.

Mind you, this little, old, gray-haired woman didn't "invent" anything – she merely "discovered" a wonderful power, which has existed ever since the first man was created.

Thanks to this discovery, we may enjoy the rights to which every normal human being is entitled, if we will!

We mention this discovery last because we believe it to be the greatest discovery of all!

What mere mechanical contraption can compare with the discovery of a power through which we may banish fear, worry, poverty, crime, and disease?

You are the equal of any human being. Your mind is bright and active. Your body is strong and healthy. Your eyesight and your hearing are perfect. You have a fair schooling. You may step into a public library and use the information collected by learned men who have gone before you, on any subject.

Yet you worry and fret over imaginary troubles which exist nowhere except in your mind! You worry for fear you will lose your position. You fret because you are not getting the salary you would like, or because your business isn't growing as fast as it should, or because you haven't as much money as you want.

You worry because all people do not agree with you. You fume and fuss because your employer doesn't run his business the way you believe he should.

You despise those who do not believe as you do concerning religion. You hate your next-door neighbors because they are "foreigners," born where your forefathers came from.

You are unsuccessful and unhappy! There are millions of others just like you, all searching for happiness, just as you are doing.

The road that leads to happiness has its beginning so close to where you are this very moment that you may not see it. The beginning is in your heart and brain, where you may lay hold of it if you will!

Each one of us must discover this road for himself! No one can discover it for us.

But there is a rule to follow which leads us to this discovery. It is this:

Look upon the world as a mirror in which you may see an exact reproduction of your true self, just as you are. Having this true likeness as a model, you can so reshape yourself that you will look to the world just as you wish to look. That's the first step.

Now, draw a picture, in your imagination, of the person you desire to be. If your desire is strong and persistent, you will soon see yourself resembling this imaginary picture which you have drawn. You will reflect this picture in those around you and they, too, will see it.

Let us suppose that you wish to become a successful salesman. You wish to have your customers see in you a magnetic personality. You wish them to follow your suggestions. You wish them to purchase your wares and come back for more. You wish to retain their friendship. You wish them to have faith and confidence in you.

How are you going to bring about this condition? Why, that's easy to answer!

First, you are going to understand that the world sees in you just what you really are. You are going to understand that the way to build other people up so they will admire you and have confidence in you is first to build yourself up so you will admire and have confidence in them!

You are going to understand that other people "sense" thoughts, moods, and feelings, and when you understand this early, you are going to think only such thoughts and have only such feelings toward others as you wish them to have toward you.

Just as surely as the electric vibrations travel out from this wireless sending apparatus and are caught and registered on a properly attuned instrument thousands of miles away, so are your thoughts "sensed" and registered by those with whom you come in contact.

Skepticism begets skepticism – hatred begets hatred – doubt begets doubt – and just as surely does love beget love – and faith beget faith.

An employee hates his employer and immediately his every act and his every facial expression telegraphs his thoughts to the employer and his fellow employees.

An angry person, so science has discovered, throws off enough poison with every breath he expels to kill a guinea pig. Anger and hatred not only pollute your mental machinery, but they poison your physical body as well. Just as a drop of aniline will color a whole barrel of water, so will an angry thought show itself in your every act and in your very face. It will not stop there, but it will reach out and inoculate those around you.

Until you learn to see something good in every human being both friends and foes, you'll never discover the Road to Happiness!

When doubt, worry, fear, skepticism, hatred, and distrust creep into your mind, the Road to Happiness becomes invisible.

> **G** **GITOMER NOTE: Negative thinking and negative expressions block creative thinking and positive thought.**

You are searching for this Great Highway, right now! Before you look any further, first decide just where you wish it to lead you. Picture in your mind the objective – the final goal you are striving to reach. Then, through the power of strong desire, concentrate all your efforts on that objective until you reach it.

Remember, the Road to Happiness leads in only one direction, and that is through the field of service to humanity! The Road will be brighter and traveling easier if you take others with you on your journey.

Your Road to Happiness may lead you into a successful business or profession. It may lead to a Sales Managership, a Corporation Presidency or a partnership, but remember that you can shorten the distance through useful service to humanity.

Cordially and sincerely yours,

Napoleon Hill

Napoleon Hill
80 East Randolph Street
Chicago, U.S.A.

ⓖ GITOMER'S THOUGHTFUL ACTIONS

HOW TO IMPLEMENT THIS LESSON

As you can see and learn from this lesson, as you look at yourself
and for yourself, everything is a choice. You choose which road you
take, and who you seek to become. My recommendation is choose
the road that leads to what you love. And surround yourself with
people who support you and think the same. Hill deals eloquently
and insightfully on the choices between happy and unhappy.
Choose happiness and positivity as your number one objective, and
everything else will fall into place. Also note that this (maybe by
coincidence) is "lucky" lesson 13. Why? Because the harder you work
at what you love, the luckier you will become.

"The road that leads to happiness
has its beginning so close to where
you are this very moment that you
may not see it. The beginning is in
your heart and brain, where you
may lay hold of it if you will!"

– Napoleon Hill

"To become a successful man is to develop mentally. You cannot stand still or retrograde, and stay in this business. It just naturally won't let you! You have to continue growing."

– Napoleon Hill

Lesson Number

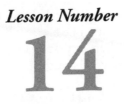

14

"LUCK versus P-LUCK!"

(An after-the-lesson visit with Mr. Hill)

G GITOMER INSIGHT: This is a 100-year-old true story that could have happened yesterday. And it could have happened to you, IF you were willing to take action. Read this carefully and ask if the hero could have been you.

A few weeks ago a young man was riding home in the smoking car, on an Illinois Central Railroad train.

The car was "dingy" as most smoking cars are, and poorly lighted, as all Illinois Central suburban cars are. Only three dim yellow gaslights were burning. A porter came through the car and turned out one of these.

Twenty-five or thirty businessmen were seated in the car trying to read their evening papers. The action of the porter made them angry – naturally! You could see that, from the expressions on their faces.

One big, red-faced, hale, and hearty red-faced fellow who sat in the seat with the young man, said to him, "Too bad somebody doesn't do something about these poor lights." "Yes," said the young man, "it is too bad, isn't it? Well, tomorrow somebody will do something about it!"

Then he stood up and made a little talk to his fellow passengers, telling them of the conversation he had just had with the man who shared his seat. He wound up suggesting that they all join in a movement to "do something" about the poor lights.

Right then and there was born a Citizens' Committee, with the young man as leader and Chairman.

The next day the young man called the President of the Illinois Central Railroad Company (by invitation) and made vigorous representations to him concerning the poor lighting system of his railroad car. The President refused to promise immediate relief.

That night four men were stationed at every downtown station of the I.C.R.R., and 20,000 passengers received handbills, calling for the assistance in forcing better service.

The next day letters were addressed to Aldermen in the city of Chicago, calling for their cooperation in passing suitable ordinances for the improvement of lighting systems on I.C.R.R. trains operating within the city limits.

By the end of the week Governor Lowden had been interviewed by this young man, for the purpose of enlisting his aid, through the State Public Utilities Commission, in improving lighting systems on I.C.R.R. trains operating in the State of Illinois.

The *Chicago Tribune* and the *Chicago Daily News,* two of the largest daily papers, took up the fight against the Illinois Central Railroad Company.

Through letters, telephone calls, and personal visits, men and women who use the Illinois Central Railroad trains got into communication with this young man and promised to cooperate with him.

A Citizens' Committee called on him and invited him to become a candidate for the State Senate.

He became known overnight almost, to the two and a half million people who constitute the population of the City of Chicago.

One of his admiring friends called him on the telephone and said – "Congratulations on account of your good luck!"

Ye gods! Luck!!

This admiring friend left off one letter. It was p-luck instead of luck. He merely used his "think box" instead of his wishbone.

When that big red-faced fellow, who shared his seat in the smoking car that night, looked up and sighed – "someone ought to do something about it," this young man agreed with him. But he didn't stop by merely agreeing – he decided to be that "somebody."

Friend, this narrative is worth remembering, because someday you'll have your chance to be "that somebody."

> When opportunity bangs at your door so hard that she almost breaks in the panels, do not say "somebody ought to do something about it!" Instead, say, "I'll be that somebody myself." And you can do it!

The young man that I refer to stands at the threshold of a roadway that leads into politics, if he chooses to enter this field.

Not by luck, but because he "made an opportunity" out of what would have seemed to the average man only idle gossip, by a fellow passenger.

The young man I refer to is an advertising man. Through his work in this field he has learned to analyze men and things. His mind has become keen and alert for detecting opportunities.

This is one of the beauties of the great work you have begun. It teaches you to be analytical. It gives you a quick grasp of environment. It causes you to unconsciously study cause as well as effect.

It makes of you a keen student of human nature. It enables you to sense the "opportune" time for action. It causes you to become enthusiastic over everything you undertake. It gives you self-confidence, hope, faith, persistence, and stick-to-it-iveness.

To become a successful man is to develop mentally. You cannot stand still or retrograde, and stay in this business. It just naturally won't let you! You have to continue growing.

You are glad that you began this course. You have already seen a big improvement in yourself. So have I. So have all of us who are guiding you over the rough spots. We have grown in proportion to the extent to which we have helped you grow.

One of these days you will be a successful Sales Manager. You will own your own home. You will drive your own automobile. Your family will have all the necessities of life and many of the luxuries. You will have a neat little bank account that will constantly grow.

Then some big red-faced fellow will come along and say – "Isn't he lucky!" Oh yes, "he was lucky" all right. When you hear of it you'll say – "poor simp" – and drive on to the bank to deposit your day's "income."

Cordially your well-wisher,

Napoleon Hill
Director of Education
George Washington Institute
Chicago

G GITOMER'S THOUGHTFUL ACTIONS

HOW TO IMPLEMENT THIS LESSON

Doer or non-doer – which one are you? Forty years ago I was riding in the car with one of my most admired mentors: Mel Green, Founder of Advance Process Supply. At the time, Mel had the most successful textile equipment and supply business in the world. I was lucky enough to have befriended him, and, through the value I offered him, be treated like a son. It was early in the freezing cold Chicago winter morning. Sleet was blowing sideways as we headed for a morning breakfast meeting. Mel had just finished launching an ink product that was so successful they couldn't produce it fast enough. I said, "Mel, you're amazing. Everything you touch or produce turns to gold. You're the luckiest person I have ever known." Without a second of hesitation he responded with words of wisdom I call on every day, "Jeffrey, hard work makes luck."

If you're looking to succeed beyond your wildest dreams, the formula is simple:

"Find something you love, believe that you will succeed, and work harder than you believe possible. The result will take you all the way from success to fulfillment."

– Jeffrey Gitomer

"Watch your helpers, then, to see that they do not fail you. Imagination has already done part of his work. Desire has performed his part. But you ought to watch Enthusiasm, Self-Confidence, and Concentration. If they fail you, your building will suffer."

— *Napoleon Hill*

Lesson Number

IMAGINATION, DESIRE, ENTHUSIASM, SELF-CONFIDENCE, AND CONCENTRATION

(An after-the-lesson visit with Mr. Hill)

G GITOMER INSIGHT: These title words are all great, and all-encompassing individually. Hill manages to intertwine them and goes deeper into the challenge of what you are made of as he defines each word. What's at your core, and how can you improve your principles and desires to achieve greater heights and success? And to fully understand the genius of this lesson, a closer look must be taken at the times in which they were written: 100 years ago. "Mental drive" was at the core of Hill's teachings and achievements – no computers, no airplanes, no TV, no smartphones, and not many paved roads. Napoleon Hill stood at the threshold of personal development and leadership, and challenged everyone he met to get better, get happier, get focused, work hard, and know in your heart-of-hearts and mind-of-minds, that you're going to win.

I suspect that these are five of the greatest words in the English Language. They are the brick and mortar out of which you may build a successful career.

Imagination is the architect through which you will draw plans for your success building.

Desire is the foundation stone with which you must start your success building.

Enthusiasm is the dynamic force which will keep your architect at work. It will permit no delays until your plans are drawn to the finest detail.

Self-Confidence is the boss-carpenter that will keep your other forces at work.

Concentration is your contractor and builder – the overseer of the boss-carpenter and all the other forces – the purchaser of materials and supplies.

Your building has been started. You have called it Success. Now watch out to see that no cheap materials are used, and that all your forces perform honest, efficient work.

You have the last word. And who are you? Why are you the owner of the building, when completed? You are the person who pays the bills for the materials and the labor which go into this new building you are constructing.

You are the final overseer of the whole job.

Watch your helpers, then, to see that they do not fail you. Imagination has already done part of his work. Desire has performed his part. But you ought to watch Enthusiasm, Self-Confidence, and Concentration. If they fail you, your building will suffer.

This is an important building that you have begun. It's no mere wood-shed. It ought to be a permanent building, and it will be if you'll be careful of its construction. It will bring you an income that will supply you with all that you need or can use in this world.

It will provide you with the four material possessions which nearly every normal person wants, namely –

1. **A home built on a little spot of ground that you can call your own.**

2. **An independent income in a business you can call your own.**

3. **A bank account that will grow into a nest egg for use when you are ready to quit active business.**

4. **An automobile.**

Oh, yes! And there is something else which your Success structure will provide, if you build it properly and that is –

AN OPPORTUNITY TO SERVE HUMANITY AND MAKE THAT PART OF THE OLD GLOBE WHERE YOU PASS ALONG A LITTLE BETTER THAN YOU FOUND IT!

Don't be a quitter! Anybody can be that, and many people are. When you lay down on the job, the boss-carpenter and the contractor and builder become indifferent and the other forces go on strike.

You've got to complete this building. There's a good reason why you must complete it. Maybe several of them. I can't tell you just what these reasons are. Perhaps the gray-haired mother who brought you into the world. Perhaps some sweet-faced little codgers of your own – already here or to come. Perhaps the sweetheart for whom you have been waiting. Maybe all these put together.

You can complete this building, and you will! You are not going to allow any negative forces to creep in, slip a bit into your mouth, and harness you to a toilsome clerkship.

You are going to harness yourself to only one thing just now, and that is Ambition! It will drive you to complete that wonderful building you have begun. It will not allow you to stand still, turn back, or quit.

It is only the weakling who permits the devils and imps to creep in and rout his self-confidence and ambition!

You are no weakling!

The personal Analysis examination which you passed successfully and with a high average, has told me this. I know more about you than you imagine I do.

I know you are not the type which gives up in despair. If you had been, you probably wouldn't have been admitted for this course. No, you are no quitter!

I believe this, with all my heart. I shall continue to believe it.

Now you be sure to think as well of yourself as I think of you!

You are entering a great profession – one that has by no means reached the apex of its greatness. There is an economic reason for the existence of the profession which you are entering. As a builder of sales and merchandising plans, you will be no human parasite. The money you earn will not be taken away from what someone else has already produced. It will be your share of what you have helped to create.

The economic distribution of the world's merchandise is one of the big problems of your time. It is becoming a bigger problem as competition increases.

The part which you play in solving this great problem may be no small part. That, however, will depend upon how well you develop your co-workers – Desire, Imagination, Enthusiasm, Self-Confidence, and Concentration.

As you go through this course, we will teach you all we can concerning the mechanics of Success. We will teach you to use that wonderful laboratory reposing in your head. Then, within a short while you will be able to draw upon this laboratory for all the constructive sales plans and ideas that you need.

You will get out of this course just what you put into it. This in spite of all that your instructors can do. Inspect carefully the materials which you put into it.

The big purpose back of the George Washington Institute is to teach men and women to think accurately. Toward this end we are constantly searching for material which will aid us in our work.

Today I read an editorial in the *Chicago Examiner* that is full of food for thought. I will quote it, but first let me describe the picture which accompanied it. In the center was a great dinosaur (an extinct prehistoric animal, said to be the largest species that ever inhabited the earth). On one side of this great animal was a modern man, and on the other side was an ape-man. At the animal's feet, so small it could hardly be seen, was a mouse. The editorial was headed:

GREATER CHANGES WILL COME.

This picture is to make men think. It shows the strange and powerful, huge and tiny, complicated ways in which nature's force has worked at the great earth problem.

That problem is to find and develop the right kind of living creature to develop and rule this earth, which is one of a great family of planets that travel through infinite space with our sun, brother in infinitude of all the distant stars.

As this little planet is the brother planet to gigantic Jupiter, as our sun, a million times the size of this earth, is the little brother of another sun one billion times bigger than our sun, so the tiny mouse in this picture is the brother of the huge dinosaur. Both are children of the same creative force.

And the ape-man at one end of the dinosaur has in his thick skull, back of his low forehead, a spark of planning intelligence that finds its brother in the brain of the more highly developed man at the other end of the dinosaur.

Through millions and millions of years this development of life has gone on.

At first, life took a form invisible to the naked eye. By the accumulation of endless billions of single cells through the process of evolution, the huge dinosaur, too big for survival was formed.

Every kind of creature nature's force made and tried. Let them pass before the eye of your mind.

The huge whale, a hot-blooded animal dwelling in the cold ocean, the creatures that fly, at the first like serpents, now some with feathers, some with fur like the bat.

The armadillo, covered, protected like the nut by a thick shell; sluggish sloths, living upside down; ants forming civilized nations; ant-eaters licking up entire ant nations at one meal; worms that live in the ground; turtles and serpents that crawl upon it; oysters fastened to the rock, unable to move; jellyfish that float where the tide takes them; sponges that are neither animal nor plant, and other creatures half-plant and half-mineral; moles that bore through the earth; eagles that go above the clouds; elephants with a trunk that is almost a hand, the most intelligent creature next to man; giraffes built to eat from treetops; swine built low to root in mud – strange, marvelous products of nature always struggling, always changing, always seeking that which is new and better, even as each of us creatures individually struggles and seeks for the new and the better.

How strangely these creatures come from the nothing that bewilders us into passing life, then go out again to that which we do not understand.

Some are created by the splitting in two of the parent creature. That is the simplest kind of new life – a piece breaks off and lives in its turn.

Next comes the egg in which life mysteriously starts. Sometimes the egg is hatched within the mother and the creature born living.

Sometimes the egg is laid in its shell, then hatched by the sun's heat or the mother's body.

Some creatures, like the ornithorhynchus of Australia, are half bird and half animal – the head of a duck, body of a muskrat.

Some mammals, like kangaroo, give birth to their young half-formed, then carry and nurse it inside of a pouch, a marsupial bag, sort of second womb, in which the half-formed creature is completed.

Always, as we read animal history in traces left in rocks and in clay, we seem to see a great blind force struggling, striving, experimenting. Some creatures are made too tiny and weak to survive; others, like the dinosaur, too huge and ungainly to compete with; others so monstrously savage the earth cannot endure or support them.

It is as though we saw a blind man modeling in clay, acting under blind impulse.

Yet we know that a fixed plan beyond our feeble understanding goes through it all.

For as we study the unborn child from the day of its conception to the day of its birth, we see repeated embryologically all the forms of life, all the processes through which living creatures on the earth have passed.

Six weeks after its life starts, the human being unborn cannot be distinguished from very low forms of life. Later, before its full development, it has the feet, the body of an ape. Before its birth that which becomes a human being goes through the whole process of life on the planet.

This picture may well inspire awe, wonder, reverence. The same force made all these things. The great and the tiny, the murderous brute savage, the so-called "civilized man," great fern trees whose dropping pollen formed the coal beds that heat us and the oil that carries us in our automobiles.

The thought as you look at this picture, dinosaur and tiny rodent, ape-man and civilized being, is this:

The marvelous changes that have gone before during millions of years past are to be followed by changes more marvelous in the millions of years that are to come.

We know that our planet, warmed by the sun and balanced by its power, will travel through endless space for hundreds of millions of years to come, and that there will be upward constant change, no going back, steady improvement. Then at some day, hundreds of millions of years distant, the sun's heat and the earth's heat will die away. Our planet and our solar system will die, as individuals die. The life of the planet and sun will move on to some future destiny, as does the life of the individual laid in the grave and apparently returning in the new-born infant.

What will the changes of the future be? Some slight but not important changes in bodily form. There will be no more dinosaurs, no winged serpents flying through the air. All the monster forms have come and are disappearing. Nature ends her animal experimenting with man's supremacy.

Man will rule on the planet alone, ever changing, but with the change INSIDE, not outside. His skull will become bigger and rounder, more symmetrical, his jaw smaller as he gets away from his biting custom, his body lighter, thinner, more powerful and active. The great change will go on in the millions of brain cells in THE REAL MAN within the skull.

A great English naturalist said, "The difference between a highly developed civilized man and a low savage is greater than the difference between that savage and the blade of grass," and he told the truth.

The greatest differences in nature's building are not those that you see in this picture. The difference between a mouse and a dinosaur is not so great as that between an ordinary human being and Shakespeare.

And the difference between Shakespeare or Michelangelo and the blade of grass is not so great as will be the difference between those "great men" of our savage period and the really great men that will come in the millions of years that lie ahead of us.

This earth will be inhabited by men that will make of it one beautiful garden, a magnificent park in which they will live, devoting their brains to the study of the outside universe, of the power that controls all things.

The new-born infant cannot talk to or learn from those that bend over its cradle. This new-born planet cannot talk to the other worlds or learn from them.

But it will not be so always. The coming race that will live here will talk to the older planets and learn from them. Individual minds unborn will have power to grasp and understand the purpose and construction of a solar system as easily as we understand the wheelbarrow.

Man will control heat, climate, and weather on this earth as easily as he controls the heat and the ventilation in a modern apartment house. The power of the tides and of the sun will be the only servant.

There is a day coming in which our descendants, happy men, will look back upon us, our selfishness and cruelty in peace, our bloodthirsty wars, as we look upon this ape-man that killed his neighbor, cracked open his thigh bone and ate the marrow.

It hath not been shown what we shall be!

If you doubt, ask yourself what this ape-man would have said had you predicted to him the flying machine, submarine, or public school.

A truly splendid editorial that you have just read. One that will cause any man to think, and anything that will do this is worth reading.

However, there is something lacking about this remarkable editorial. When I have read it I want to ask:

"What solution do you recommend? What can I do to hasten this happy day of greater enlightenment of which you write?" It makes me feel as if I had read almost to the climax of a fascinating story and then closed my book without knowing how the story ended.

Now I shall not presume to improve the work of the great writer who wrote this editorial, nor do I wish my suggestions to be construed as a criticism of his splendid, thought-inspiring work, but I shall write a short climax such as I would have given this editorial had I written it. In doing this it is my aim not only to give you something additional to think about, but also something to do that will speed the day when "man will control heat, climate, and weather on this earth as easily as he controls the heat and ventilation in a modern apartment house."

Man is superior to all other animals only in one particular, and that is in the power to think. He is not the strongest animal physically, by a great deal, yet is master of all other animals because of this superior power of thought!

This, within itself, ought to suggest the nature of the climax that I shall write for this editorial. But, if it does not, let me suggest that if thought is the quality which distinguishes man-power from brute-power, is it not likely that man can achieve still greater power by learning to think more accurately?

Go back and read lesson three again, particularly that portion of it which tells how to think. Get the simple principles therein stated clearly fixed in your own mind, then explain them to at least a dozen other people, particularly your own children if you have any.

Get fixed in your mind the scientific fact that every thought reproduces bodily action and has a strong tendency to crystallize into physical reality if kept in the mind long enough.

Acquaint yourself with the scientific fact that thoughts which dwell upon fear of other men actually place you in the ape-man classification and give the more powerful and courageous man who thinks complete power to drive you as though you were an ape.

Get clearly fixed in your mind the feeling of joy and happiness which comes to the man who has supplanted hatred, doubt, and skepticism with love, faith, and belief in humanity. Understand the scientific fact that you cannot fully enjoy the peace and quietude of the man who loves humanity until you have learned to love all humanity!

If you wish to master your enemy, learn the power of forgiveness and deal him a crushing blow by extending him the hearty handshake the next time you meet.

And when your enemy looks startled and surprised at your sudden change of heart, notice how he, too, will supplant his hatred with forgiveness. You will be master of the situation and the more powerful because you have learned to think and make use of Nature's laws.

Finally, the definite thing that you can do right now to contribute your part toward hastening the day of greater enlightenment is this...

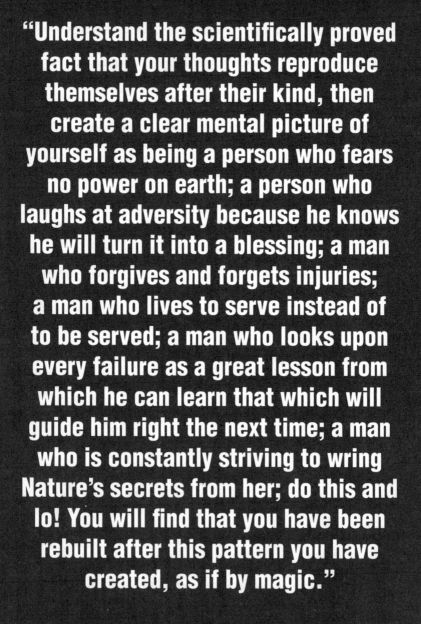

"Understand the scientifically proved fact that your thoughts reproduce themselves after their kind, then create a clear mental picture of yourself as being a person who fears no power on earth; a person who laughs at adversity because he knows he will turn it into a blessing; a man who forgives and forgets injuries; a man who lives to serve instead of to be served; a man who looks upon every failure as a great lesson from which he can learn that which will guide him right the next time; a man who is constantly striving to wring Nature's secrets from her; do this and lo! You will find that you have been rebuilt after this pattern you have created, as if by magic."

– Napoleon Hill

Then, after you have performed this miracle on yourself, teach others how to do the same. The principle is simple and results sure –

Merely focus the mind upon the mental picture of the condition you wish to create, of the person you wish to be, and Mother Nature does the rest, in time.

– Napoleon Hill

By practice you can become so adept at transforming thought into physical reality that you can do it almost instantly.

Man never has and never will build anything in physical or mechanical form that was not first created in thought form. Get that clearly fixed in your mind and prove it to your own satisfaction by trying to think of something that man created which was not first created in thought.

Remember that the information out of which you create thought reaches your mind through the five senses of seeing, hearing, smelling, tasting, and feeling.

Remember that information may be true or untrue, and that the accuracy of your thought will depend upon the accuracy of the information which reaches your mind.

Remember, also, that prejudice is the arch enemy that stands guard over your five senses and often "colors" information so it is untrue when it gets to your mind.

Become an accurate thinker, then follow your thoughts with action and you will place yourself a thousand years ahead of ninety percent of the world's population, in the evolution of man.

Cordially your friend,

Napoleon Hill
80 E. Randolph Street
Chicago, U.S.A.

G GITOMER'S THOUGHTFUL ACTIONS

HOW TO IMPLEMENT THIS LESSON

I love this lesson the best so far. It's so inspirational and at the same time, it's as informative as one can possibly absorb. To convert these strategies into today's world, you have to think about "what was" and FOCUS on "what is." For example, Hill's take on "CONCENTRATION/FOCUS" is much harder now than when Hill wrote about it 100 years ago – we have phones pinging us with people, information, texts, and multiple forms of communication. And at the same time, TV and advertisements are all over trying to grab your attention. Hill challenges you about SELF-CONFIDENCE AND CONCENTRATION and then talks about how focusing the mind will affect your actions and success. Use a timer to see how much time a day you're focused on sales and success activities. All five of these elements are equally significant: imagination, desire, enthusiasm, self-confidence, and concentration. Please look at each one personally and introspectively. How can you take these five words and positively put them into your thinking and your life? The key to implementation is writing down your thoughts about each word, then defining the present situation in your life, and finally making a plan to improve (with a deadline to measure against).

Lesson Number

16

Who is BEHIND your success?

(An after-the-lesson visit with Mr. Hill)

G GITOMER INSIGHT: The word "advertising" used in this lesson is both real-world and metaphoric. And please do not be offended by the slight political correctness imperfection – that's what life was like 100 years ago (and it was totally acceptable to all back in 1917). It has certainly been proven over the past few decades that women are not the "weaker" sex. In fact, especially in my home of four daughters, four granddaughters, and a girlfriend, quite the opposite is true. The brilliance of this lesson is that often others see qualities in you that you cannot see about yourself.

If this lesson pushes the limit of what you would consider today as "politically correct," get over it and seek the lesson beyond Hill's words. It's all about who is supporting you and speaking up for you as you seek success.

If you are a married man, this little after-the-lesson talk is for your wife. If you are a single man, it is for the woman whenever you find her. If you are a married woman, it is for you for his benefit. If you are a single woman it is for you for his benefit after you get him.

"We all need a source
of inspiration. We need
someone to gently urge
us to achievement,
and when we find
the person who is
interested in us enough
to do this, we ought
to stick to that person
as a drowning man
would cling to a
floating straw."

— *Napoleon Hill*

A few weeks ago, a little thin 110-pound woman ushered a big, strong, healthy 275-pound husband into my office. I could tell from the sheepish grin on his face that he was being brought against his will. He looked "hen-pecked," poor fellow. Furthermore, I could see that he wanted my sympathy.

The little woman did the talking. She was keen, alert, and business-like in her manner.

She said, "I've brought my husband in to see if you'll accept him in your class. He has been working as a street car conductor, but I've decided he can do something better than that."

The big stiff looked at me and winked.

The little woman went on with her story. She told of her ambitions to raise and educate their four children. Of her longing for life's necessities for her little brood.

The heavy-weight sat there and grinned. For the ambitious little woman's sake, I put him through the usual psychological tests. He showed about as much ability for advertising work as a Jackrabbit.

The first thing we do in analyzing an applicant who suspects that he is afflicted with the latent "Advertisingitis" ability is to get at the motive which prompted him to turn his attention toward his field. We do this because we have found it quite easy to develop advertising ability in a person who has first set his or her heart on becoming an Advertising Manager, while the task is much harder where the student wants to take up the work just because of the belief that it will provide an "easy berth."

Well, in the case of our heavy-weight friend I thought it best, for obvious reasons, to remove him from the influence of the "menacing wife," so I conducted the examination in private. As soon as we were alone, he told me frankly why he came to see me (I listened just as though I didn't already know).

He said, "My wife got this here fool notion in her head to make me git into this advertising game. It was them confounded advertisements you've been running in the papers. Why, man, that woman hasn't 'lowed me to git a decent night's sleep for two weeks on account of this."

I said, "Never mind, old chap, I understand. I'm married too!"

But – and then I let him have it! I delivered the old boy a solar-plexus knockout blow that he will never forget.

I told him that he was the most fortunate man I had ever analyzed, out of over 10,000 cases, and I meant every word of it! Fortunate because he had someone to believe in him and urge him on to success!

This fellow was about 38 years of age. He had never done anything but manual labor. I found upon further investigation that he had been through high school, although his "jargon" didn't indicate it.

He was a bright fellow in many ways, but as a whole he was an "impossible."

But what impressed me was the way that faithful little woman was fighting to fire him with ambition.

Somehow, I couldn't keep from telling that fellow what I thought of him. He didn't like it. That was the only encouraging sign that I saw. He showed some signs of anger when I opened up on him and told him what I thought any other man would do under the guidance of that ambitious little wife of his.

I asked him if he had ever heard that Andrew Johnson was taught by his wife to read and write, and that largely through her influence he became Vice President of the United States.

"Yep" – he had heard about it!

We all need a source of inspiration. We need someone to gently urge us to achievement, and when we find the person who is interested in us enough to do this, we ought to stick to that person as a drowning man would cling to a floating straw.

It is very seldom that we find all the ambition with the "weaker" sex. More often it is the wife who lacks imagination sufficient to build castles in the air. Not because she lacks ambition, in most cases, but because she never stops to think what a wonderful power she can become in her husband's life, if she will but urge him on and encourage him to be more by undertaking more!

The richest blessing to which any man can fall heir is an ambitious wife who will encourage him, fill him with hope, faith, ambition, and self-confidence.

We all need this support. Someone to tell us that we are doing good work. Some men get along without it, but have you ever undertaken to estimate how much better they would get along with it?

I tell you we need this mental stimulant. We may believe that we are doing good work, but we know we are if a trusted friend tells us so. We all like to have our own opinions corroborated.

There is absolutely no estimating what a normal man can do with the hearty, loyal cooperation of an enthusiastic, ambitious wife.

Lucky is the man who has one. With such a life partner you may set your goal as high as you wish and achieve it!

The greatest blessing any man ever enjoyed is the companionship of a cheerful, serene, ambitious wife who constantly urges him on to greater achievement. She may preside over a humble little household, but there you will find order, harmony, and an inviting environment. A place where ideas will sprout and grow.

If I live to be a hundred years old, I shall never forget the man who first placed his hand on my shoulder and said –

"Nap – you're a bright boy!"

Those were the sweetest words I had ever heard, perhaps because I had never heard them before.

That very moment the seed of ambition was sown in my heart and brain. It has never let me rest since.

That chance remark made, perhaps, in a half-jocular spirit is directly responsible for the splendid time I am having with you who are studying with us. Had they never been spoken, I might have been forever deprived of the sudden development which I am enjoying from my humble efforts to help you and the others who are studying these lessons.

Let me leave this thought with you: If you are the wife and your husband is taking this course, start today – right now – to supply him with new inspirations and encouragement. Believe in him and let him know it. This is one story that truly never grows old. In a short while you will see a wonderful change in the man who is to build your fortunes.

Do not allow him to become self-satisfied! That's the sort of man who still holds down a clerkship when the silvery hairs put in their appearance.

If you are a wife-to-be (and we have many of them with us), remember this little "visit," after the partnership has been formed.

And if you are a man who has not yet selected the life partner, be careful that you pick out one whose aims and ambitions are at least as high as your own, and higher if possible.

Then, after you get her—or probably before, blue-pencil a few of the sentences in this visit and leave it around where she will "run across it" some time.

When the big fellow left my office, his face bore a different expression. He looked a bit more business-like than he did when the little woman ushered him in, half an hour before.

As they left she asked: "Do you believe he will ever become an advertising man?"

I nodded toward the big fellow and replied, "Ask him what he thinks about it." I didn't have the heart to tell the truth.

As I rang for the elevator I saw her place her handkerchief to her eyes. I felt like doing the same. But that big fellow was one in ten thousand, and that little woman was one in a hundred thousand. Maybe there will be a street car wreck one of these days and then she may have an opportunity to sow the seed of enthusiasm and encouragement where it will take root and grow.

Who can tell?

Earnestly your friend,

Napoleon Hill

Napoleon Hill

P.S. Mrs. Hill has just finished reading the above. She suggests that this medicine is good for both man and woman. I suspect she is right. Well, anyway, it will not hurt either one to try it.

🄶 GITOMER'S THOUGHTFUL ACTIONS

HOW TO IMPLEMENT THIS LESSON

> ## "If you want to be successful, surround yourself with successful positive people."

– Jeffrey Gitomer

The key to putting this lesson into your life is to cultivate great friends and associates who know you well, and want you to succeed. Maybe even help you to succeed. People who are willing to encourage you and speak positively about you in your presence and absence.

To find and gain favor from people who are willing to bet on you just as much or more as you are willing to bet on yourself. People will bet on you, IF YOU'RE WILLING TO BET ON YOURSELF and YOUR SUCCESS.

"And you could never guess what I decided upon. It was not wealth! It was not even health! It was not the country estate that we have been planning. No, it was none of these, but something more fundamental than all of them put together..."

— Napoleon Hill

"Ponder well before you decide, for you may live to realize it!"

— *Napoleon Hill*

Lesson Number

17

IF I HAD BUT ONE WISH!

(An after-the-lesson visit with Mr. Hill)

Ġ GITOMER INSIGHT: Ever wish for something outrageous? Of course you have. The question is: Did the wish come true? The answer is: Rarely, if ever. In this lesson, Hill asks you about the IMPACT your wish coming true would make on your life and the lives of others. You know the expression, "Be careful of what you wish for"… Hill says to be CERTAIN of what you wish for, and calculate the outcome when it comes true. Read carefully, Hill's ONE WISH will surprise and inspire you.

On Sunday mornings, I usually go out into the parks and mingle with nature. All during the week I must talk to men and women concerning business, but on Sunday mornings I talk to the trees and to the beautiful blue waters of Lake Michigan.

And you might not believe it, but they talk back to me. I draw from them enough inspiration to tide me over a hard week's work.

On these Sunday morning walks – and especially when I go alone – I plan ways and means of helping you and our other students.

A few Sundays ago, as I enjoyed my usual ramble among the trees along the lakefront the "small still voice" asked me what would be my wish if I had but one and it could be instantly fulfilled.

If you believe this is an easy question to decide, stop right now and try it on yourself!

At first I thought of great wealth, and of all the good I could do if I had Rockefeller's or Carnegie's millions. I thought of all the advantages I could give my two boys and my wife. I thought of the sights we might see as we traveled around the world, and of the pleasure it would give me to come home and write all our students about my trip. I thought of the beautiful country home for which we have been planning.

"Yes," said I to myself, "wealth is the thing!"

But somehow this decision didn't seem to satisfy me. I felt that there must be something more desirable than mere dollars. I sat down on the trunk of a willow tree which had grown out over Lake Michigan, and dangled my feet just above the water's surface. As I sat there I went back to first causes and analyzed wealth. I carefully studied those who have accumulated vast fortunes as a result of having performed a useful service to mankind. Then I studied those who have come into fortunes by inheritance, without having performed any service of use to mankind.

I was beginning to get near the basis of my "first wish."

And you could never guess what I decided upon. It was not wealth! It was not even health! It was not the country estate that we have been planning. No, it was none of these, but something more fundamental than all of them put together.

My wish was – THAT I MIGHT BE BLESSED WITH GREATER KNOWLEDGE OF THE HUMAN MIND – MUCH MORE KNOWLEDGE THAN HAS YET BEEN DISCOVERED OR USED

– THAT I MIGHT UNDERSTAND THE HIDDEN POSSIBILITES OF NATURE'S LAWS WHICH CONTROL THE

GREATEST OF ALL WEALTH-PRODUCING MACHINES, THE HUMAN MIND, and particularly MY OWN MIND!

- THAT I MIGHT LOOK JUST A LITTLE BEYOND THE PRESENT SPHERE OF HUMAN ACCOMPLISHMENT AND UNDERSTAND THE NATURAL FORCES OF THE AIR, SUNSHINE, AND DARKNESS.

- THAT I MIGHT UNDERSTAND NATURE'S LAW THROUGH AN INTELLIGENT OPERATION OF WHICH WE MIGHT HARNESS AND USE THE FORCES OF GRAVITY MORE EFFECTIVELY – THROUGH WHICH WE MIGHT EASILY UTILIZE THE SURGING ENERGY OF THE ROLLING WAVES OF THE OCEAN – THROUGH WHICH WE MIGHT HEAT OUR HOUSES, COOK OUR MEALS, AND OPERATE OUR INDUSTRIES BY HARNESSING THE SUN'S RAYS IN THE DAYTIME AND THE MOON'S RAYS AT NIGHT.

IN SHORT, MY WISH IS FOR MORE KNOWLEDGE AND LESS IGNORANCE CONCERNING THE WORKING MATERIALS WHICH GOD HAS PLACED HERE FOR OUR BENEFIT. FOR WITH THIS GREATER KNOWLEDGE WOULD COME ALL THAT WE HUMAN BEINGS NEED ON THIS SIDE OF THE GREAT DIVIDE!

What would your wish be?

Ponder well before you decide, for you may live to realize it!

Very cordially yours,

Napoleon Hill
80 East Randolph Street
Chicago, U.S.A.

🇬 GITOMER'S THOUGHTFUL ACTIONS

HOW TO IMPLEMENT THIS LESSON

Try Hill's idea. Make a wish – not too outlandish – and then work for it to become a reality. Small begets big.

Think about where Hill was and how inspired his thinking was. Now think about your thoughts and your ONE WISH. Hill was able to have such great thoughts in this moment because he was inspired (by nature), calm, happy, and relaxed. Note: He was also getting some exercise. Think about how and when you get your best thoughts. Only in the shower? If that's the case then you need more relaxed thinking time.

On a personal note, I have one wish besides peace, health, wisdom, happiness, and harmony for my family. *I wish for the health, strength, and mental faculties to write ten more books before I turn 100.*

But this is about YOU. I challenge you to write down your ONE WISH, then revisit it when you finish the book and put together a plan to accomplish it. Think it. Write it. Take action to achieve it.

Lesson Number

18

THE GREAT MAGIC KEY

(An after-the-lesson visit with Mr. Hill)

G GITOMER INSIGHT: Hill is going to talk about the magic key to success. What do you think it is? Well, here's a clue: YOU ALREADY POSSESS IT! It's just underutilized. Hill will show you in a few short pages how to turn it on and keep it well oiled. WARNING: Do not take this lesson lightly. He's not just telling you what to do, he's telling you, "This is how I do it!"

In presenting to you this "Great Magic Key," let me first explain that it is no invention of mine.

It is the same Key that is used in one form or another, by fellow men of Mental Science and New Thought. I have separated it from religion and occultism, and have attached it to plain everyday business procedure.

This Great Magic Key is a most wonderful power, yet perfectly simple of operation. So simple, that most people have failed to make use of it. We human beings are too prone to look askance at so simple a formula for success, a formula which will open the door for health and wealth; yet, such a formula is the Great Magic Key.

It will unlock the door to riches! It will unlock the door to fame! And in many cases it will unlock the door to physical health. It will unlock the door to education. It will let you into the storehouse of all your latent ability. It will act as a pass-key to almost any position in life you may choose.

Through the Great Magic Key we have unlocked the secret doors to all of the world's great inventions. Through its magic powers all of our great geniuses have been produced.

We will suppose that you desire a better position in life. The Great Magic Key will help you attain it! Through its use Carnegie, Rockefeller, Hill, Harriman, Morgan, and Guggenheim have accumulated millions of dollars in material wealth.

It will unlock prison doors and turn human derelicts into useful, trustworthy human beings. Out in the Arizona State Prison at Florence, Arizona, is Louis Victor Eytinge, a "lifer." When the prison gates closed behind him, he was a concrete specimen of the worst that the human race produces. Tuberculosis had reduced him to a skeleton, physical and moral depravity had reduced him to the bottom of the scale mentally. Then came the touch of the Great Magic Key. Eytinge made use of it. Today he is one of the leading men of the world. He is repaying the debt which he owed. He has grown in both physique and mentality until he is now sound in both. He overcame tuberculosis. He choked off his bad moral tendencies. Now he is ready for a pardon and the world is ready for his useful service, outside of prison walls.

You ask – "WHAT IS THIS GREAT MAGIC KEY?"

And I answer with one word: CONCENTRATION!

To stop here would be insufficient. You must know how to use this Great Magic Key! First let me tell you that AMBITION and DESIRE are the great dynamic powers which you must summon to the aid of CONCENTRATION. Without Ambition and Desire, the GREAT MAGIC KEY is useless. That is why so few people use the Key.

"DESIRE whatever you may, and if your desire is strong enough, the GREAT MAGIC KEY of CONCENTRATION will help you attain it."

– *Napoleon Hill*

DESIRE whatever you may, and if your desire is strong enough, the GREAT MAGIC KEY of CONCENTRATION will help you attain it. If the object of your desire is something which is humanly possible to attain.

Study the great accomplishments of the followers of Mental Science and New Thought. The dominating power back of these is CONCENTRATION plus DESIRE! There are learned men of science who would have us believe that the wonderful powers of prayer itself operate through the principle of CONCENTRATION and a strong DESIRE backed by unyielding faith.

I am making no attempt to either associate or dissociate the story of the Great Magic Key with occultism or religion. I am treating it from the ordinary everyday layman's viewpoint. I am dealing with it from actual knowledge I have gained in carefully analyzing and charting over 10,000 people. I am frank to confess that I know little of the origin of the powers back of CONCENTRATION or DESIRE. But I do know a great deal of the effect of those powers. I have seen them demonstrated to my own satisfaction hundreds of times. We will assume that you are skeptical of the powers of CONCENTRATION and DESIRE. Let's put these to the test, through a concrete example.

First, you must do away with skepticism and doubt! No unbeliever ever enjoyed the benefits of these great powers. You must believe in the test which I am going to ask you to make. You must let no feeling of unbelief creep in.

Now we will suppose that you have thought something about becoming a great writer or a great public speaker, or a great business executive, or a great manager. Suppose we take the latter as the subject of this test. But remember that if you expect results, you must follow instructions to the letter.

Take a plain sheet of paper, ordinary letter size, and write on it in large letters – the largest it will carry – these words:

I AM GOING TO BECOME A GREAT PERSON!

BECAUSE THIS WILL ENABLE ME TO RENDER THE WORLD A USEFUL SERVICE AND BECAUSE IT WILL PROVIDE ME WITH THE NECESSARY MATERIAL THINGS OF LIFE!

I WILL CONCENTRATE ON THIS DESIRE FOR TEN MINUTES DAILY, JUST BEFORE RETURNING AND JUST AFTER RISING.

_____

(Sign your name)

If you are not good at lettering, just clip out the foregoing, sign it, and place it where you will see it just before retiring and just after getting up each day; do exactly as you have pledged yourself to do, for at least ten days.

Now, when you come to do your "CONCENTRATION," this is the way to go about it: Look ahead three, five, ten, or even fifteen years from now. See yourself in a position paying a big salary. See the happy faces of your loved ones – maybe a wife and babies – maybe a mother with silvery hairs.

See yourself laying aside a nest egg for a rainy day. See yourself in your motor car which you will be able to afford. See yourself in your own cozy little home that you will own.

See yourself a person of influence in the business world. See yourself INCREASING IN VALUE EARNING STILL MORE MONEY as you grow older. See yourself engaged in a line of work where you will not fear the loss of a job. Paint this picture through the powers of your imagination and lo! it will turn into a beautiful picture of DESIRE. Use this DESIRE as the chief object of your CONCENTRATION, and see what happens!

If may take longer than ten days. Again, it may take only one day. That will depend upon how well you perform the task.

You now have the secret of the Great Magic Key! It will unlock the door to whatsoever position in life you want if that position is humanly possibly of attainment. It will make of you a better employee and a better citizen if the object of your concentration is a worthy one.

Use this Great Key with intelligence! Use it only for the attainment of worthy purposes, and it will give you the things of life for which your heart may crave. So simple, so easy of application, yet SO MARVELOUS IN RESULTS! Try it! Begin right now. Forget the mistakes you have made in the past. Start all over again, and make the next five or ten years tell a story of human accomplishment in whatever line of work your calling may have placed you, that you will not be ashamed of – that the generations of your family yet to come will be PROUD of!

MAKE A NAME FOR YOURSELF THROUGH – AMBITION, DESIRE, IMAGINATION, AND CONCENTRATION!

Finally, I wish to leave this thought with you. It has been my constant companion through life. It has supported my tired legs when they would otherwise have allowed me to fall by the wayside. It is this:

"EVERY ADVERSITY IS IN REALITY A BLESSING IN DISGUISE. THE UNIVERSITY OF HARD KNOCKS IS THE GRANDEST SCHOOL IN THE WORLD. IT SENDS ITS GRADUATES FORTH TO FIGHT LIFE'S BATTLES. ABLE AND STRONG ENOUGH TO OVERCOME EVERY OBSTACLE THAT MAY CONFRONT THEM."

"From every failure
we may learn a
great lesson
if we will."

— Napoleon Hill

Let me summarize the five chief points in this series of lessons, so you will not forget them. They are (1) Self-Confidence, (2) Enthusiasm, (3) Working with a "Chief Aim," (4) Performing more work than you are paid for, and (5) Concentration, backed by desire and unwavering faith. By a reasonably intelligent application of these qualities, you can become master of your own career.

Very cordially yours,

Napoleon Hill

Napoleon Hill
80 East Randolph Street
Chicago, U.S.A.

🄖 GITOMER'S THOUGHTFUL ACTIONS

HOW TO IMPLEMENT THIS LESSON

Hill loves to use the word "magic" because it conjures up the idea that you must master the magical aspect of your career and craft by perfecting the ordinary. Hill guides through the thought process and gives you the steps – but only YOU can do the work.

Think about a time you were going through a hardship. Write down what happened and the lessons you learned. Write down what you are now choosing to do differently as a result of the event. Now think about your blessed successes, and go through the same process. The reason for documentation is obvious. It's your success journal and your success journey. CONCENTRATE ON YOU!

Lesson Number

19

THE VALUE OF PERSONAL APPEARANCE IN CREATING A FAVORABLE FIRST IMPRESSION

(An after-the-lesson visit with Mr. Hill)

 **GITOMER INSIGHT: WARNING: DO NOT TAKE THIS LESSON LIGHTLY.**

Hill's colleague O. H. Chamberlain, Jr., himself a world-class salesman and business leader, is given the opportunity to talk about the importance of first impressions people and salespeople make, and the impact those impressions can make both personally and financially. The warning is: do not think that your first impressions are OK until you have talked to others.

I gladly relinquish my pages for this lesson to Mr. O. H. Chamberlain, Jr., whom I consider to be one of the leading salesman of America. Mr.

Chamberlain brings to you, through this little visit by proxy, the benefit of his experience, in a managerial capacity, with such well-known firms as the National Cash Register Company, The American Multigraph Company, and others of equal prominence.

Mr. Chamberlain will talk to you, through these "sacred" pages of mine, on the subject of –

"THE VALUE OF PERSONAL APPEARANCE IN CREATING A FAVORABLE FIRST IMPRESSION."

It is ordinary business custom to give a man of good personal appearance a courteous reception.

The most inconsiderate men do this, if only for selfish motives. They fear that they may turn away a possible patron.

Until a man is known, the things which go to make up his personal appearance are the credentials which entitle him to courtesy. A cordial greeting is a good start toward securing a satisfactory interview, which launches a salesman toward his goal.

Another reason for cultivating a pleasing personal appearance is that the average business man has many demands upon his time. Often it is not possible for him to grant every request for an interview. He chooses those to whom he will give attention. Naturally, he chooses those whose personal appearance pleases him most.

A sale is the process of changing a prospect's mind from inattention and indifference to complete accord with the salesman's mind. It is accomplished only by creating certain impressions in the prospect's mind.

An impression is a favorable impression when it adds its ever-so-little power to turn the prospect's thought in the right direction. Mental impressions are created both through the senses and by the reason.

The first impression which the prospect receives from the salesman is through his sense of sight. It will be favorable or unfavorable just in proportion as the appearance of the salesman is pleasing or displeasing. It is a law of mind that every impression is colored by the preceding ones. Therefore, it is of primary importance that the first impressions be pleasing.

A graceful and easy carriage denotes strength. The average man does not know how to walk, stand, or sit. Children should be taught early in life the proper carriage of the body so that unconsciously they may be at ease.

A man's bodily attitude is a mirror which reflects his mind and spirit. The slouching man has a slouchy mind. Self-respect, authority, and assurance manifest themselves as unmistakably in the carriage as do servility and self-depreciation.

No man whose carriage shows indecision, doubt, or carelessness will impress a stranger favorably. The attitude of the healthy man, sitting, standing, or walking should be erect. It is nature's sign of well-being.

I recently witnessed a clear illustration of the two extremes of carriage. During the inauguration of a western governor, he was attended by several stout policemen and a spruce young orderly. Throughout the ceremony it was distressing to watch the discomfort of the policemen. Standing on their flat feet, with stomach extended and chest collapsed, they shifted from one foot to another. The aide-de-camp stood at attention throughout the entire ceremony with no sign of discomfort. He rested easily on the balls of his feet, stomach thrown in, chest held high and forward, and head thrown back.

The carriage of the salesman, as he walks forward to greet his prospect, should betoken health and courage, faith in himself and in his mission. If he is invited to take a seat, he should not collapse into the chair, sink down in it, and sit on the point of his back bone. He should sit erect, though not stiffly. For the salesman, like the orderly, is a soldier – a vanguard in the army of modern commerce.

The impression that he is talking to a vigorous, self-respecting man is certain to influence the prospect.

The salesman's dress has much to do with creating a favorable first impression. It should be suited to his business. If it is too foppish or too slovenly, it will divert attention from his mission. It should be adapted to the season and startling effects should be shunned.

Lord Chesterfield says that a man is best dressed when those who behold him have no sense of his apparel except that of a perfect whole.

A man need not be expensively clothed in order to be well dressed. Clean linen, well-brushed and pressed clothes, a fresh tie, and shoes well shined contribute much to the well-dressed man.

Poise plays a large part in appearance. The prospect instinctively looks at the bearing and facial expression of the salesman. If he sees there the serenity and mental peace which poise brings, he unconsciously relies on them.

The eyes of the man of poise are good to look into. Optimism or pessimism indelibly stamps its story upon the features. Disease and health reveal themselves through the face. The serene soul alone is strong.

The absence of bodily and mental control is shown in mannerisms. Many salesmen have failed because of irritating eccentricities. At best, the mannerism detracts from the maximum attention and interest on the prospect's part. He cannot attend to the salesman's language, however logical and convincing it be, if it is accompanied by fidgeting and lack of ease.

There are mannerisms of the body: swaying, wriggling, and constant changing of position. They should be overcome. Many salesmen have characteristic ways of holding their heads. Unconsciously, they wag them from side to side, shake them, throw their heads back and forward, or run their hands through their hair.

There are mannerisms of the feet, shuffling, tapping on the floor, sliding, and unconsciously kicking against a chair or desk, which preclude that attention on the part of the prospect which the salesman desires.

Many mannerisms of the face hinder a thoughtless salesman. In his desire to give emphasis, a salesman sometimes will extort his facial muscles to an extent which is very disagreeable to his auditor. Some men seem unable to find a place for their hands. They are continually moving, stopping now and then to let the fingers tap the "devil's tattoo" on the top of a desk or the arm of a chair. One of the most disagreeable mannerisms of the hands is the "washing in invisible soap and water," as if in imitation of an English butler.

An unpardonable breach of politeness is putting the fingers in the mouth and biting the nails. Fondling the head and face with the hands should be avoided, as it is not only an evidence of lack of ease, but prevents your auditor from hearing you distinctly.

Above all, do not handle objects on the prospect's desk. Some men resent the liberty, and, in any case, it shows lack of self-control.

It should not be necessary to point out that the salesman should keep his hair well trimmed and brushed, his nails manicured, and his face shaved. Yet many men are limiting their earning power today by neglecting just such essential details of persuasive appearance.

Nothing is negligible in salesmanship, however small it may be, if it affects a sale. The salesman who creates an unfavorable impression by hands, neck, and face in need of scrubbing, finger nails in mourning, or dandruff upon his coat is greatly handicapping himself.

The salesman should constantly guard his breath. Nothing will repel a prospect so surely as foul breath.

The test of a salesman's progress, from the time he enters another man's place of business until he leaves, is in drawing the other man toward him. Any impression which repels should be guarded against, whether it be in personal appearance, speech, or action.

The real test is this – will it attract or distract the prospect? Will it win or lose his interest?

Very cordially yours,

Napoleon Hill

Napoleon Hill
80 East Randolph Street
Chicago, U.S.A.

ⓖ GITOMER'S THOUGHTFUL ACTIONS

HOW TO IMPLEMENT THIS LESSON

Look at yourself in the mirror. First impression is not just the impression you make on others. It's the impression you give to yourself. How are you dressed to read this book? Dressed with a "ready to win" spirit? What kind of impression are you making every day with your customers, your colleagues, your family…yourself? Unsure? Take a selfie every day. Ask people around you who you trust, and who make a good first impression every time. While your appearance may not help you win the sale, bad appearance could cause you to lose the sale.

Lesson Number

20

AT THE SIGN OF
THE DOLLAR

(An after-the-lesson visit with Mr. Hill)

G GITOMER INSIGHT: This lesson is another pivotal point in the book. Hill distills his insight and wisdom in a succinct and flowing way so that most of you are lulled to sleep – except for a few – those few that grasp at what Hill was saying will receive the reward of the century – oh wait – they already did. Be as astounded at Hill's genius as I was.

Well, here I am back with my shovel and spade ready to dig in my "sacred garden spot" again.

I feel very lonesome when I turn over these pages to someone else, even for one lesson.

This is a suitable point in your course at which to leave with you a thought which I do not want you to overlook. I have seen doctors who made a practice of leading their patients to believe that they were very sick, largely because with this thought came the natural expectation of paying a big fee.

To come to the point quickly, permit me to say that I do not believe in this practice. I believe that self-confidence is the state of mind which precedes success. I believe that all great truths are, in their final analysis, very simple. In furtherance of this belief, I want to repeat again that the mechanics of success and achievement are not the most important part of the work which you are preparing yourself to do. It is your DESIRE to be able to execute the principles I have laid out.

However, the important part of every man's success is to create the plan back of the philosophies. You who are preparing yourself as professional men and women must be ever alert and on the lookout for short cuts.

It is but an incident that your salary is drawn from some particular employer. Your real salary is paid by the consumer of the commodity which the company offers.

For many years the Oliver Typewriter Company has been marketing its machines at $100 each. It has been selling through the usual plan of distribution through agents.

Just recently it has cut off its entire agency force and gone direct to the consumers with the machine at $49 each. At one stroke, it has clipped off 50% of excess baggage which the consumer has heretofore been compelled to shoulder.

> **G GITOMER NOTE: Sound familiar? This was written 100 years ago. Read on…**

Just now, the question of the High Cost of Living is occupying the attention of the entire world. The man or woman who creates a plan for shortening the route between producer and consumer on any commodity is well on the road toward success in the field of selling.

If this were the last "after-lesson visit" I ever expected to have the pleasure of writing for you, I would devote the space to the subject which I have selected for this time. I would urge you, to the utmost extent of my power, to shorten the route in every way possible between the producer and the consumer. Under our present distribution plan, we have loaded the consumer with altogether too much excess baggage. In many cases he is paying a profit to the producer, jobber, wholesaler, and retailer, whereas he ought to pay a profit only to the producer.

Some of you may be engaged in the retail business. Others of you are or will be working for the retailer. Others working for the wholesalers and jobbers. Let me say to you who feel that this argument is striking close to your source of bread and butter, that a readjustment of our distribution plan is bound to take place. There is an economic necessity for this readjustment. I am warning you now so you may get ready for the time when this readjustment must materialize. If you are going to become a top-notcher in the field of Success and Selling, you must keep your mind at work over-time devising ways and means of delivering at least the necessities of life to the consumer at a less cost. This is your great problem, students of sales and success. It always will be your great problem.

Master the mechanics of sales as we are teaching it, yes – but also begin right now to cultivate the viewpoint of the consumer. Study his needs as well as those of the producer. The big sales men and women of the future – those who command $10,000, $15,000, $25,000, or even $50,000 a year – are going to be the men and women who will devise ways and means of supplying the consumer with the necessities of life with fewer middlemen's profits tagged on.

It makes no difference how close to home this argument may strike you, the logic of it cannot be evaded. To be forewarned is to be forearmed. Commence now to adjust yourself to the new economic era which is rapidly rising above the horizon of commercial progress.

Over one hundred million dollars a year in business is coming here to Chicago to the one firm of Sears, Roebuck & Company. Anywhere that you place the point of a pin on the map in the United States and in many of the foreign countries, you will find regular customers of Sears, Roebuck & Company.

Why is this?

The answer is that Sears, Roebuck & Company is supplying the consumer with merchandise at a less cost than it can be purchased for after it has gone through the hands of several middlemen.

Some of these days, someone is going to win both fame and fortune by devising ways and means of going a step further than Sears, Roebuck & Company have gone. This person, whoever he or she is, will work out a plan which will bring merchandise to each local community where it may be first examined and then purchased at mail-order prices. The plan, when it is perfected, will be very simple. That is, it will sound simple enough after someone has made a few million dollars of profit out of it.

Think for a moment what an enormous buying power a concern would have if it did all of the buying for one store located in each town and city in the United States. You can very readily see where Sears, Roebuck & Company's business would go if such a plan were perfected.

G **GITOMER NOTE: Hill has just predicted Wal-Mart and Amazon in one sentence.**

Somehow or other I cannot help feeling that this plan, when it is worked out, will be credited to some of my students. This is something for you to think about. Talk it over with your local banker. Talk it over with your local merchants. Get all the information on the subject that you can. And bear in mind always while you are discussing this subject that the big problem in merchandising today is the problem of economic distribution – the shortening of the route between producer and consumer.

Bear in mind also, that the great mass of people are demanding at least the necessities of life at a lower cost than they are now paying. If you can help solve this problem, even on one commodity, you can write your own salary price tag.

Earnestly your friend,

Napoleon Hill

Napoleon Hill
Director of Education
Bryant & Stratton College
CHICAGO, U.S.A.

(Copyrighted, 1917)
Napoleon Hill

G GITOMER'S THOUGHTFUL ACTIONS

HOW TO IMPLEMENT THIS LESSON

Is this an amazing prediction of the future or what? Hill just laid out the game plan of Amazon and Wal-Mart. And did it accurately and eloquently – 100 years ago.

Sears grew tremendously in Hill's time from 1900 to 1960, and now if you're under the age of 20, you may never have even been in a Sears. Why? They, like Kmart and Borders, refused to change with the times. They refused to or could not develop new distribution models and new sales channels.

DO NOT get complacent and comfortable like they did. The world is ever evolving – evolve with it. Invent and reinvent your business and your endeavors based on your customers' needs.

"Success may be had by those who are willing to pay the price...And the price is eternal vigilance in the development of Self-confidence, Enthusiasm, Working with a Chief Aim, Performing more Service than you are paid for, and Concentration. With these qualities well developed you will be sure to succeed."

— Napoleon Hill

Lesson Number

21

"THE FIVE-POINT RULE"

(An after-the-lesson visit with Mr. Hill)

Ⓖ GITOMER INSIGHT: This lesson contains more golden nuggets of truth for your success as a person, not just a career person. Hill gives examples of people who believe, for whatever reason, they can take shortcuts to success and knowledge. All the people who took shortcuts failed. But more important, Hill refocuses on the five principles that will build success and knowledge.

This seems a mighty appropriate place to again call your attention to the thought which we have tried so hard to implant in your mind from the very beginning of these lessons: "THAT YOU WILL GET OUT OF THESE LESSONS EXACTLY WHAT YOU PUT INTO IT IN TIME AND PERSISTENT EFFORT."

That is a thought worth remembering!

It is a thought that applies to everything you undertake throughout your entire life. If you get nothing more from your course than this one thought, and you make proper use of it, you will be well repaid for your time and money.

A gentleman of wealth once took his son to the dean of a well-known university of whom he inquired, "Can't my son finish his university course in less than the prescribed four years?"

The dean replied, "Well, that depends upon what you want him to be. For example, you can grow a squash in one summer, but it takes a score of years to produce an oak tree. If your son wants to become a squash he can squeeze through in two years, but if he wants to become an oak tree he will have to take more time."

A young man came to me to be analyzed. He had a notion that he wanted to get into the $10,000-a-year class. He was all excited over the thought of holding down a big position. At the time, he was working as a stenographer. He wanted to take up advertising, right away, quick! Said he, "Ought I not to be making at least $5,000 by the end of next year?" I replied, "Yes – you OUGHT to be, but – YOU WON'T BE!"

He thought it strange that I would "discourage" him by such frankness. I told him that I made it a point never to discourage anyone from doing the right thing, but that I believed it wise to discourage a person from building air-castles on false foundations. I had just finished reading Bruce Barton's editorial, which appeared in the March 18th, 1917, edition of *Every Week* magazine. It made my meaning quite clear, and the young man got my point very forcefully. That editorial is worth repeating. In it you will find a great lesson if you will stop and think of it in the right light. I recommend that you read it, not ONCE, but MANY TIMES!

Here it is:

"Generally Speaking, a Job Is Good in Proportion to the Amount of Study Required to Master It."

Yesterday morning, when I rode up in the elevator, the starter was breaking in a new elevator-boy.

At noon when I went out to lunch, the new boy was running the car alone. He had on a uniform, and was starting and stopping with the confidence of a veteran.

From apprentice to professional in a couple of hours.

Last week I saw a veteran motorman breaking in a youngster. On Tuesday and Wednesday the two were on the front platform together; on Thursday, the new man was operating the car alone.

It is a sight I have seen very often, yet I never see it without feeling of wonder.

What thoughts are in that young fellow's head as he receives his instructions from the gray-haired veteran?

How can he fail to look forward and see in the older man a picture of himself twenty years from now?

He is taking up a low-paid job – a job with no future. Twenty years from now he will be just where he is today – only older, with a grasp on the job somewhat less secure. His experience will count for nothing, because it is experience that any other man can gain in a couple of days.

He may, by walking out on strike, force an increase in his pay of a few cents a week. But the increase will not be large. Why?

Because he learned the job in two days. And in any other two days, the company can get plenty of men who will learn just as fast and take the job away from him.

On the same day, I met in a hotel restaurant a friend of mine who had just come back from England after taking special work in surgery under some of the greatest men in the world.

He is thirty-one years old; it is fourteen years since he entered college.

For ten of those fourteen years he has been in medical schools, in hospitals, and in foreign countries studying.

The rest of us – his classmates – have been in business ten years. He has in all that time never been able entirely to support himself. Always his education was costing him a little more than he earned.

Yet with what result? He has acquired a specialized training such as only a few other men in New York possess.

He will begin his life with an income of several thousand; he will pay back his educational debts in a couple of years; in ten years, his income will be tens of thousands.

It took him fourteen years to master his profession. But he need have no fear of losing what he has gained. No other man can displace him, except at the cost of fourteen years of work.

I have nothing but sympathy for the old man who finds himself condemned for the rest of his life to a no-account job. But I find it hard to be patient when I see young men blithely dancing into jobs with no future, simply because they are too lazy to fit themselves by study for jobs worthwhile.

Every young man in the United States ought to read the autobiography of Benjamin Franklin. See with what painful diligence he taught himself to write good English. Watch him at fourteen, attacking again the arithmetic that he had three times failed to pass in school, and conquering it.

See Michelangelo, old and blind, still being wheeled into the great galleries, that he might with his fingers trace the outlines of the statuary – still true to his life's motto: Ancora impara *– "Still learning."*

"The gods sell anything to everybody at a fair price," said Emerson.

And when he said it, he epitomized the philosophy of Business.

The job that the gods sell for two hours' training is worth just what it costs.

Only that job is worthwhile which has tied to it the price tag of constant, unceasing study and work.

— Bruce Barton, Editor

The older I grow, the more I realize the good, sound philosophy which the foregoing editorial contains. Persistency is a wonderful quality. We get in about the proportion that we give, no matter what we are engaged in. That's a great lesson which most of us need to learn over and over again before it STICKS! Those who bet on the "ponies" learn – sometimes – that we cannot get something of value for nothing.

Those who play the stock markets learn the same lesson – sometimes! Go wherever you will, follow whatever vocation you choose, but in the final end, when the LAW OF COMPENSATION gets in its work, you will find that you will "reap that which you sow."

Success may be had by those who are willing to pay the price. And most of those who crave a $10,000-a-year position – especially if they are engaged in business – may realize it if they will pay the price.

And the price is eternal vigilance in the development of Self-confidence, Enthusiasm, Working with a Chief Aim, Performing more Service than you are paid for, and Concentration. With these qualities well developed you will be sure to succeed.

Let's name these qualities the "FIVE-POINT RULE."

Earnestly your friend,

Napoleon Hill

Napoleon Hill
Director of Education
80 East Randolph Street
Chicago, U.S.A.

🅖 GITOMER'S THOUGHTFUL ACTIONS

HOW TO IMPLEMENT THIS LESSON

It's never too early or too late to learn. I dropped out of college at age 20. At the time I thought I knew everything. I decided to travel in Europe for a year. When I got there, I realized I knew nothing. After the first week of my yearlong journey, I dedicated myself to lifelong learning with the specific mission of learning one new thing every day. That was 50 years ago, and I've been learning (and implementing that knowledge) ever since.

Having never written commercially until I was 46 years old, and having never spoken professionally until I was 47, and having never published my first book until I was 48, I consider it all a blessing. Not to have achieved this — oh no, quite the contrary. My blessing is from my dedication to study personal development, observe to understand, develop positive self-confidence, concentrate on and complete the task at hand, and have the burning desire to both serve others and achieve for myself. That's a blessing.

Why not take some personal time to sit alone and focus on YOU! Write to yourself. What have you achieved? Where are you now? And what do you need to do to get to your desired outcomes? Now is a good time to review the five qualities named in the Five-Point Rule and rate yourself on how good you are at each quality. Then write down what and where you need to do to improve. Now is a good time to focus on YOU – deeper concentration – deeper dedication – deeper desire. It's time for you to create a deeper dedication to learning and earning.

"You will never know the real joy of living until you come into a full understanding of the Principle of Service."

— Napoleon Hill

Lesson Number

22

THE PRINCIPLE OF SERVICE

(An after-the-lesson visit with Mr. Hill)

G **GITOMER INSIGHT:** There is a 5,000-year-old Chinese proverb that says, "To Serve Is to Rule." "Service" is at the heart of Hill's philosophy. Hill loved to serve and from his earliest writings was an advocate of "render more service and better service than you are being paid for." This lesson defines the process and the principle, and puts service where it belongs – on the top of the list.

I am writing on the fifteenth day of June, nineteen hundred and seventeen. Last night our resident class held its commencement exercises at the Chicago Advertising Club. More than one hundred people were in attendance at this farewell meeting. It marked the closing of the hardest year's work I ever performed, yet I hasten to add the statement that it has been my most profitable year – profitable from every viewpoint.

I have thrown every ounce of energy that I possessed into this work. Many have been the nights that I have gone home so exhausted that I couldn't sleep. But the task has been performed. Our first year has been an overwhelming success. We have accomplished even more than we started out to accomplish a year ago. I frankly confess that I do not covet another such responsibility as I have carried in building this course, yet I do not regret the price I have had to pay. It was the only way this course could be built. Now that the first year's work has been finished, the task during the ensuing years will be comparatively simple.

Throughout this course, I have done my utmost to implant in the minds of my students the Principles of Service upon which the course is founded. I have exerted every ounce of energy in establishing the truth that SERVICE RENDERED is *cause* while the PAY ENVELOPE is *effect*! I have tried my best to show my students that they will GET in exact proportion what they GIVE!

My own work has been a splendid exemplification of this Principle. When I look back over the past year's work, these points stand out against the horizon of my experience so clearly that I deem it worthy to mention them:

First: I have worked harder than
I ever worked before.
Second: I have been happier
than I ever was before.
Third: I have done more for others
than I ever did before.
Fourth: I have profited more
financially, and have grown bigger
mentally than I ever did before,
in the same length of time.

But this is no surprise to me. I anticipated these results long before we even began this course. I have traveled far enough along life's pathway to familiarize myself with the particular law of nature through which these results have been accomplished. I have long since learned that plenty of wholesome work – work into which we can throw our whole hearts and souls – work which helps others to grow and succeed – is absolutely essential for our own happiness and success.

I have also learned beyond the slightest question of a doubt that when we begin to help others, we begin also to help ourselves; that in proportion to our SERVICE to the world do we ourselves succeed.

> # I have learned that with the rendering of great service to the world comes financial reward sufficient for all our requirements, and in proportion to the service we render!

THAT IS THE GREATEST LESSON OF ALL!

It is a lesson that I want every one of my students to learn! You have heard it mentioned in previous lessons. You will hear it mentioned many times in subsequent lessons. I wish I might be gifted with the power of a Billy Sunday or a Dwight L. Moody or some of the other great preachers. If I were, I would preach the Principle of Service from one side of this old earth to the other. I would be perfectly willing for others to give you Eternal Salvation, and content myself with teaching you how to be happy and prosperous while on this earth.

What lies beyond the Great Divide none of us know. Your opinion on that subject is as apt to be correct as mine or as that of the greatest preacher that ever lived or ever will live!

What I want and what I shall do my best to help every one of my students acquire, is knowledge that will help us here, on this old ball of mud, right now, while we live! As far as we know, the only good we can do must be done while we live. And, if I do not err in my judgment, the greatest good we can possibly do is that of making life's journey as pleasant as possible for as many people as possible. Personally, and speaking in a broad, general way, that is my CHIEF AIM in life; I have been part of the fulfillment of that CHIEF AIM, I have been for many years, and still am, preparing myself as a writer, philosopher, and teacher.

Before I can write, philosophize or teach effectively, I must understand and apply the Principle of Service.

This I am striving to do, and the more I learn about this great Principle, the stronger I become as a teacher and philosopher. In passing on to others what little I have learned of this Principle, the more I find I am learning about it myself.

YOU CANNOT GIVE WITHOUT GETTING!

But I fear I am soaring in the clouds. Let me come down to earth and give you a concrete illustration of what I mean, stated in every day plain English: As I have stated, I have worked harder during the past year than I ever worked before. I have given myself and the little that I have learned in the University of Hard Knocks, freely and willingly. I have given without any thought as to monetary returns. On two occasions during the past year I have been offered positions at salaries far above any figure that I ever anticipated being able to earn. Both of these offers came from men who are at the heads of two great corporations, and both men were unknown to me until they approached me. It happened that a member of my class was Secretary to one of them. The other one heard of me through one of my magazines in which we advertise. Both of these men had been watching my work for several months, and one of them had visited my class without my knowledge of his identity. They caught the spirit of the Principle of Service which I have been teaching. They saw how beneficial that spirit would be if properly injected into their organization or workers, and the bids for my services followed.

I refused both offers! It was the biggest temptation to lay down that which I had commenced that I ever experienced. It took courage and belief in the work in which I am engaged to turn away an offer of a salary two and a half times as big as one ever made before.

I say to you, just as I said to one of these men when I refused his offer, that no sum of money can tempt me to turn away from the work which I have begun. This school must become the biggest and most beneficial school ever conducted for the purpose of helping men and women master their ambitions in the field of commerce and industry. That sounds rather extravagant – I'll admit that it does! It sounds that way to me and probably it does to you– but it must be realized.

The first step toward this realization has been taken. We have both feet on the ground, ready for the next step. I have at least thirty years of active service ahead of me. All of those thirty years shall be devoted to the task which I have begun. During every one of those years we shall send forth some hundreds of bright men and women, each of whom will become an active preacher of the Principle of Service. We sent out more than one hundred such people the first year; people who felt, for the first time perhaps, abundant self-confidence, enthusiasm, and determination to accomplish a definite objective, in a definite way. All of these people believe in us – they are giving back to the soil a part of that which they took away from it by encouraging others to come to our school. In all parts of the United States, right now, we have men and women who have felt the benefit of our help and who are, in turn, reciprocating.

YOU CANNOT GIVE WITHOUT GETTING!

The Principle of Service works while you are asleep just the same as while you are awake. Applying this principle, as we are, we have every reason to expect to see this become the world's greatest school of personal development.

Success and Salesmanship are not all we intend to give our students. These, in fact, are but incidental. We intend to develop in our students a magnetic personality, self-confidence, enthusiasm, courage, sincerity of purpose, strength of character, persistency, and determination!

With an aim like this, what, may I ask, shall hinder us from becoming the world's greatest school?

You can help! You ought to help! Not to benefit us, particularly, but to exercise the Principle of Service and put it into action! Also, to help those who need what we have to offer – those in whom you are interested.

You will never know the real joy of living until you come into a full understanding of the Principle of Service. Try it! Give your employer a fuller measure of service tomorrow and note the increased happiness which you will enjoy tomorrow night!

Cordially and sincerely,

Napoleon Hill
80 East Randolph Street
Chicago, Illinois

🅖 GITOMER'S THOUGHTFUL ACTIONS

HOW TO IMPLEMENT THIS LESSON

When Hill says, "YOU CANNOT GIVE WITHOUT GETTING!" he means GIVE FIRST and the world will pay you back.

Of course I think of myself, and my accomplishments, as I read this lesson. You? Of course you did. It's human nature. But the question is: Who did you serve and how did you serve in the process?

Most people have a "sales plan," but very few have a "service plan."

Hill's immortal quote "Render more service and better service than you are being paid for" is at the heart of this book's philosophy. Go back to all of your writings and add a service plan to each goal or task.

But here's an easy way to make service a habit: Make a goal to perform one random act of kindness a day – and do it with a smile. This will, over time, give you a service heart – and the understanding that that is where service starts.

"Through your acts
and deeds begin
sowing seeds of
kind thoughts and
lo! they will take
root and grow
where thistles
grew before."

– *Napoleon Hill*

Lesson Number

23

A GREAT TRUTH WHICH I HAVE LEARNED FROM TWENTY YEARS' EXPERIENCE

(An after-the-lesson visit with Mr. Hill)

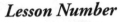 **GITOMER INSIGHT:** This final lesson is not a summary – rather it's a challenge. Like the first 22 lessons, it contains both information and the wisdom to help implement the lesson. BUT this is the most powerful lesson in the book. And keep in mind that Hill didn't "save it for last" – rather, he knew that without the knowledge from the first 22 lessons, this lesson would not have had the impact it's meant to convey. Read it. Do it.

It is Sunday morning – the day on which we should take a sort of personal inventory of ourselves to see what we have learned during the preceding six days.

I have just finished my inventory, not only for six days, but also for the twenty years which have just passed, this being my birthday.

I cannot give you all of the details of my inventory covering these twenty years, but I can and will give you the most important ones, with the hope that they will be of benefit to you. I believe it just as important to take a retrospective view of ourselves as it is to look ahead and try to anticipate what the future holds for us, because out of the great mass of mistakes which we have made we can learn a wonderful lesson if WE WILL!

Instead of telling you of a dozen or more important truths which I have learned from my experience during the past twenty years, I shall content myself with telling you of the BIGGEST, MOST STUPENDOUS, MOST WONDERFUL TRUTH THAT I HAVE LEARNED!

I shall tell you of this truth because I sincerely believe that it will aid you to live a better life, and to achieve your aims in less time and with greater satisfaction. In fact, I seriously doubt that you can either succeed or be happy without either consciously or unconsciously observing this great TRUTH!

It is not a new truth!

It is as old as the world itself, but nonetheless a truth on that account. Remember, that it is not new truths that we need to study, but the old ones which have been preached to us for so long that we have grown tired of them.

In telling you of this great truth, this GREAT LAW OF NATURE, I have no intention of trying to entertain you. The mission of this "visit" is to teach! If, perchance, it should be an entertaining nature, so much the better, but that is only an incident.

Nearly fifteen years of the past twenty years I have spent in unintentionally trying to deny this great truth – this law of Nature! Not only did I unintentionally try to deny it, but I unconsciously did so!

"Our only sin is that of ignorance."

It was through ignorance concerning the simple laws of nature that I wasted fifteen years of tireless effort in trying to do the impossible task of defying Nature's laws!

And the worst part of it all is the fact that my ignorance amounted to willful and wanton ignorance, because I had heard of this truth – this law of Nature of which I shall tell you – until I had become tired of hearing it.

I came to look upon it as being a parallel to the cry of "the wolf, the wolf!"

What is this great truth?

I will state it in the same words in which I so often heard it, but with the hope that you will make more ready and practical application of it than I did for over fifteen years. It is this:

"WHATSOEVER YE SOWETH THAT SHALL YE ALSO REAP."

It has taken me fifteen years to accept and understand the truth stated in these simple words! Fifteen years of failure, unhappiness, and disappointment!

If I can save you fifteen years of heart-breaking errors, my Sunday morning effort in writing this "visit" will have been worthwhile. Yes, if I can save you five or even one year of misdirected effort, my time will have been decidedly worthwhile.

Knowing from my own experience how vague and meaningless these words which I have quoted above may seem, I shall proceed to show you, if I can, just how the truth which they convey really affects you in everything you do.

I can best do this by citing one of the experiences which have been poured from the crucible of my own life during those fifteen years of misdirected effort.

(In taking you behind the curtains, as I shall do, and divulging to you some of the mistakes I have made, I know you will understand that I am not doing so because I am proud of these mistakes, but because of my desire to help you avoid making the same mistakes.)

When I say that I was a failure during those fifteen years, I have no intention of conveying the impression that I was ever "down and out"! For at least a portion of that time I was far from being down-and-out, and nearly all of the time I had all I needed of this world's goods and chattels, but I was a failure, just the same.

By "failure" I mean that I had unknowingly deprived myself of the greatest of all worldly possessions – the knowledge of how to be happy and how to make others happy.

MY BIG MISTAKE: Trying to GET more than the real value of the services I GAVE! The hardest lesson I had to learn was that if I sowed a crop of poor work, I must necessarily reap a harvest of small pay!

I completely overlooked the fact that the SERVICE I RENDERED WAS CAUSE, while the PAY I RECEIVED FOR THAT SERVICE WAS EFFECT. I studied the effect – the PAY ENVELOPE – long and late hours, but made the regrettable error which so many others are making of overlooking CAUSE, which is the SERVICE I RENDERED!

The "Principle of Service," as Sheldon has so well called it, is a law of Nature itself. It is immutable as the law of gravitation, and to violate it brings as sure a punishment as would the violation of the laws of gravity if you should climb to the top of a tree and jump off. In either case you will find yourself crushed as a result of either your own ignorance or, worse still, your own carelessness.

"WHATSOEVER YE SOWETH THAT SHALL YE ALSO REAP."

I now understand the great philosophy that is back of those words — those words which, for fifteen years, were meaningless to me!

Not only has my own experience convinced me of the futility of trying to evade or deny this great truth, but my observation of others convinces me that all who have truly "found themselves" have learned and made use of this same truth.

This great truth may be stated in another way:

"If you live by the sword, you will die by the sword."

As I write, being mobilized in America are millions of men and billions of dollars to bring home this great truth to an autocrat on the other side of the Atlantic who started out to rule the world by the sword some three years ago.

G GITOMER NOTE: This is a reference to World War I.

Sometimes it requires the shedding of much blood and the devastation of great fortunes to impress this truth upon those who deny it, but in the end, after the "Law of Compensation" has done its work, the truth still prevails!

Napoleon Bonaparte learned this truth, even though he seemed well on the way toward world conquership before it cut him down.

Whenever there has been strife between the peoples of the earth, the oppressors and the aggressors have learned this truth to their sorrow.

Whenever there is strife between individuals, the aggressor has learned this truth sooner or later — mostly "later"!

Nature's laws may be violated, but the violation brings sure punishment, even though it seems slow in arriving in many instances.

Go back and read the "SELF-CONFIDENCE-BUILDING CHART" which I present with the "visit" in Lesson Five. There you may find the sum and substance of the best philosophy that I have drawn from the past twenty years of experience. I particularly direct your attention to the sixth paragraph. You will do well to memorize that whole Chart and make the philosophy part of your own, but whether you do this or not, be sure not to overlook the sixth paragraph. At least memorize the second sentence in that paragraph:

"I will therefore engage in no transaction which does not benefit alike all who participate with me."

> **G̈ GITOMER NOTE: (The entire chart is available at www.HillsFirstWritings.com).**

In that one short sentence, you will find what I required fifteen years to learn! Taking the Chart as a whole, you will find that it contains all of the philosophy which any human being needs with which to succeed and be happy. In the seven short paragraphs of this Chart, as I have already stated, may be found the sum and substance of what I tried to deny for fifteen years, but which I was finally forced to accept or go through life a complete failure.

You ought to make it a part of you – not because I wrote it – but because it is the key to the storehouse of peace and plenty, happiness and success.

To GET you must GIVE! Conversely stated, you will GET that which you GIVE! To me this seems so simple, so plain and understandable that every human being on earth ought to profit by it. However, it has only been during the past five years that I have so readily accepted and made use of this great truth. Fifteen years of failure and then success, in my case, ought to give encouragement to those who have not yet learned this truth.

The curse of the human race today is the practice of trying to REAP that which was not SOWN! Nature will see to it that Nature's laws are obeyed. Enforcement of these laws is not always swift, but it is SURE!

I am not sure, but if my own experience is a reasonable criterion by which to judge, I can state with positive assurance that the only real SUCCESS is that which is attained through some sort of service that is helpful to humanity! I have done more to help others during the past five years than I did in all of the other fifteen years which comprise my business experience. I have been happier and more prosperous in every sense of the word during these five years than I was during the entire previous fifteen years.

My humble advice to you is to lose yourself in some useful service to humanity, make the "Principle of Service" a part of your philosophy, master the "Self-Confidence Chart" and make it a part of your everyday efforts, and you may safely forget everything else, FOR YOU WILL BE BOUND TO SUCCEED!

Personally, I have turned my fifteen years of mistakes into capital, because it has been chiefly through my errors that I have learned what is right. In every failure that I have made I have learned a great lesson. Out of the mistakes of the past has come the new Napoleon Hill – the man that you know through these "visits." If you have made similar mistakes, and doubtless you have, you may convert them into capital, but it will have to be done just as I have explained, by making the great truth herein stated a part of yourself.

"As a man thinketh in his heart, so is he."

Start today and make use of all that this "visit" has brought to you. If you will again read paragraph four of the "Self-Confidence-Building Chart," it will aid you in making this start. All of the philosophy, all of the laws of Nature, all of the help in the world will do you no good unless you paint a definite picture of the person you intend to be, and then proceed to transfer that mental picture into reality.

Adopt a "Chief Aim in Life,"
a DEFINITE PURPOSE, and then
accomplish that purpose through
SELF-CONFIDENCE, aided by the
great powers of Nature's own laws, as
stated in that wonderful truth
which is the subject of this "visit."
"WHATSOEVER YE SOWETH,
THAT SHALL YE ALSO REAP!"

This is the greatest truth that I have learned from my past twenty years of experience. I never expect to learn of a greater truth. Make use of it in your relations with all of your fellow men! Take it with you to work tomorrow! Try it out for yourself!

Through your acts and deeds begin sowing seeds of kind thoughts and lo! they will take root and grow where thistles grew before. Instead of nursing hatred in your heart, even for those who have been unfair and unjust toward you, plant the seeds of love and charity and see how quickly these seeds will reproduce themselves. This is the Great Law of Harmonious Attraction which Dr. Sears mentions in his splendid book entitled, *How to Attract Success*.

The world is a great looking glass in which we see, not the imperfections of others as we imagine we do, but the thoughts and acts which we create ourselves.

Sincerely your friend,

Napoleon Hill

Napoleon Hill
80 E. Randolph St.
Chicago, U.S.A.

Ḡ GITOMER'S THOUGHTFUL ACTIONS

HOW TO IMPLEMENT THIS LESSON

This lesson is both powerful and thought provoking. Not just a summation of the book, but a clear challenge to you, the reader. If you don't take actions here, go back and read this book from the beginning. If you take action to develop your "chief aim" – later renamed by Hill as a "definite major purpose," and subtitled as "the starting point of all achievement" – you will find yourself on an unstoppable path to success in any endeavor.

Now is the time to define and or refine your chief aim, and detail the steps necessary for achievement, the collaborations needed, the financial requirements, the dedication and allocation of time to be invested, the service you must provide, and of course, the expected outcome. This is a real plan – a life plan – a success plan that would make Napoleon Hill proud.

Ⓖ EPILOGUE BY JEFFREY GITOMER

The TRUTH, the Whole TRUTH, So Help Me HILL

NAPOLEON HILL: Although preceded by (and inspired by) the founding fathers of personal development: Samuel Smiles, Orison Swett Marden, George Clason, James Allen, Russell Conwell, and Elbert Hubbard, Napoleon Hill is clearly the most well-known and recognized positive attitude and achievement expert in the 20th and 21st centuries. His iconic book *Think and Grow Rich* has been, and still is, the global modern-day bible of personal development and positive thought.

With more than 500,000 interactive Facebook followers, an active and responsive Twitter audience, and millions of YouTube views, the Napoleon Hill Foundation has more than kept up with the times, maintained a daily online presence, and as a result, Napoleon Hill has remained the voice of positive attitude and personal development in the 21st century.

For the past 100 years, Napoleon Hill's writings have affected the way millions of people think, act, achieve, and prosper. He is by far, the global authority on introspective thinking, positive mental attitude, and personal achievement. *Think and Grow Rich* is the global standard for personal development, but is only one book of many in his amazing body of work. *Truthful Living* sets the foundation for all of Hill's writings.

Here's what this means to you. It's exposure to Napoleon Hill's original thinking and writing about personal development, positive attitude, and wealth.

"The world is a great looking glass in which we see, not the imperfections of others as we imagine we do, but the thoughts and acts which we create ourselves."

– Napoleon Hill

Here's why you need to reread this book again. There are so many gems in this book, it's impossible to absorb all the information and feel the impact in just one reading. Keep in mind that I read *Think and Grow Rich* ten times in one year. Repetition leads to mastery.

Here's where this helps you win and succeed…

This book is a gift and a challenge. The contents speak for themselves. The question (and the challenge) is, how will you speak them, implement them, use them, and convert them into success for yourself? Hill used them for his success. How will you convert them into your success 100 years later? Will you convert them into your success 100 years later? It is my sincere hope that you do.

Here are 12 quotes from the book to live by…

- **"First comes thought; then organization of that thought into ideas and plans; then transformation of those plans into reality. The beginning, as you will observe, is in your imagination."**

- **"Among the thousand and one little things which go to make up the qualifications necessary in the thoroughly efficient man is the all-important faculty of working with a definite purpose in view – with a "chief aim in life."**

- **"Big pay and little responsibility are circumstances seldom found together."**

- **"Enthusiasm is simply a matter of SELF-INSPIRATION, nothing more nor less."**

- **"Any idea, plan, or purpose may be placed in the mind through repetition of thought."**

- **"It seems to me that one of the great purposes of life is to BE HAPPY ALL THE TIME AND TO MAKE OTHERS HAPPY!"**

- **"God made THE world, but He doesn't make YOUR world."**

- **"Effort only fully releases its reward after a person refuses to quit."**

- "BE AMBITIOUS IF NOTHING MORE. OTHER THINGS WILL TAKE CARE OF THEMSELVES."
- "The richest experience that can come to a man or a woman is that of financial reverse. The full value of such an experience will depend upon whether we accept it as a blessing or as a curse."
- "AS A MAN THINKETH IN HIS HEART, SO IS HE."
- "WHATSOEVER YE SOWETH THAT SHALL YE ALSO REAP."

These amazing quotes are the tip of the iceberg. Go back and reread this book and you'll find 100 more. Not just quotes – thought-provoking, life-changing words of wisdom. Take them for yourself and turn them into wealth. Hill would have wanted it that way.

If you are a serious "student of the game," this book has the winning formula and the winning pieces – all you have to do is roll the dice and MOVE YOUR OWN PIECE.

– Jeffrey Gitomer
  King of Sales

"Character is built
slowly, step by step.
Your every thought and
every action go into it."

Napoleon Hill

Books You
Ought to Read

(Hill's Original Recommended Reading)

How to Attract Success, F. W. Sears, Center Publishing Company, New York City Price **$1.80**

An Iron Will, O. S. Marden, Thomas Y. Crowell Company, New York City **.50**

Obvious Adams, Robert R. Updegraff, Harper & Brothers, New York City **.50**

Thinking as a Science, Henry Hazlitt, E. P. Dutton & Company, New York City **$1.00**

Hints for Young Writers, O. S. Marden, Thomas Y. Crowell Company, New York City **.75**

The Art of Thinking, T. S. Knowlson, Fredreick Warne & Co, Twelve East Thirty-Third St., New York City **$1.00**

Do It to a Finish, O. S. Marden, Thomas Y. Crowell Company, New York City **.30**

Self-Investment, O. S. Marden, Thomas Y. Crowell Company, New York City **$1.25**

Economy, O. S. Marden, Thomas Y. Crowell Company, New York City **.35**

Not the Salary but the Opportunity, O. S. Marden, Thomas Y. Crowell Company, New York City **.35**

Getting On, O. S. Marden, Thomas Y. Crowell Company, New York City **$1.25**

Emerson's Essays, R. W. Emerson, Sears, Roebuck & Company, Chicago **.39**

"Education comes from within; you get it by struggle and effort and thought."

— *Napoleon Hill*

JEFFREY GITOMER
Chief Executive Salesman

Gitomer Defined (git-o-mer) n. 1. a creative, on-the-edge writer and speaker whose expertise on sales, customer loyalty, and personal development is world renowned; 2. known for presentations, seminars, and keynote addresses that are funny, insightful, and in-your-face; 3. real-world; 4. off-the-wall; 5. on the money; and 6. gives audiences information they can take out in the street one minute after the seminar is over and then they can turn it into money. He is the ruling King of Sales. See also: salesman.

AUTHOR. Jeffrey Gitomer is the author of the *New York Times* bestsellers *The Sales Bible*, *The Little Red Book of Selling*, *The Little Black Book of Connections*, and *The Little Gold Book of YES! Attitude*. Most of his books have been number one bestsellers on Amazon.com, including *Customer Satisfaction Is Worthless, Customer Loyalty Is Priceless*, *The Patterson Principles of Selling*, *The Little Red Book of Sales Answers*, *The Little Green Book of Getting Your Way*, *The Little Platinum Book of Cha-Ching!*, *The Little Teal Book of Trust*, *Social BOOM!*, *The Little Book of Leadership*, and the *21.5 Unbreakable Laws of Selling*. Jeffrey's books have appeared on major bestseller lists more than 500 times and have sold millions of copies worldwide.

OVER 75 PRESENTATIONS A YEAR. Jeffrey gives public and corporate seminars, runs annual sales meetings, and conducts live and virtual training programs on selling, YES! Attitude, trust, customer loyalty, and personal development.

BIG CORPORATE CUSTOMERS. Jeffrey's customers include Coca-Cola, US Foodservice, Caterpillar, BMW, Verizon, MacGregor Golf, Hilton, General Motors, Enterprise Rent-A-Car, AmeriPride, NCR, IBM, Comcast Cable, Time Warner, Liberty Mutual, Principal Financial, Wells Fargo, Blue Cross Blue Shield, Carlsberg, Mutual of Omaha, AC Nielsen, Northwestern Mutual, Church Mutual Insurance, MetLife, Sports Authority, GlaxoSmithKline, the *New York Post*, and hundreds of others.

IN FRONT OF MILLIONS OF READERS EVERY WEEK. Jeffrey's syndicated column, Sales Moves, appears in scores of business journals and newspapers in the United States and Europe, and is read by more than four million people every week.

ON THE INTERNET. Jeffrey's WOW website, Gitomer.com, gets thousands of hits per week from readers and seminar attendees. His state-of-the-art presence on the Web and e-commerce ability has set the standard among peers, and has won huge praise and acceptance from customers. Jeffrey's blog, salesblog.com, is another free resource for sales and personal development information.

BUSINESS SOCIAL MEDIA. Keep up with Jeffrey and his social media presence on Facebook, Twitter, LinkedIn, and YouTube. New ideas, events, and special offers are posted daily. With more than one million social media followers, and more than four million YouTube views, Jeffrey has built a groundswell of attraction and engagement.

ONLINE SALES AND PERSONAL DEVELOPMENT TRAINING.
Gitomer Learning Academy is all Jeffrey, all the time. Gitomer Learning Academy contains amazing interactive video courses based on Jeffrey's thirteen bestselling books with interactive questions, 25+ webinars, and hours of Jeffrey's real-world practical sales information, strategies, and ideas. It starts with a skills-based sales assessment and then offers an interactive certification course. This amazing sales tool will rate your sales abilities and explain your customized opportunities for sales knowledge growth. The online academy is available 24/7/365 on any device. It is continually updated as Jeffrey records new video lessons and content. It's ongoing sales motivation,

sales reinforcement, and personal inspiration with the ability to track, measure, and monitor progress and achievement. The minute you read, watch, or listen to any of Jeffrey's content, you can put it into immediate action and use it on your next sales call. Gitomer Learning Academy is innovative. Gitomer Learning Academy is effective. Go to GitomerLearningAcademy.com for ongoing sales motivation and personal inspiration.

SALES CAFFEINE. Jeffrey's weekly e-zine, *Sales Caffeine*, is a sales wake-up call delivered every Tuesday morning to more than 250,000 subscribers, free of charge. *Sales Caffeine* allows Jeffrey to communicate valuable sales information, strategies, and answers to sales professionals on a timely basis. You can subscribe at www.salescaffeine.com.

SELL OR DIE PODCAST. Jeffrey Gitomer and Jennifer Gluckow share their sales and personal development knowledge in their weekly podcast, *Sell or Die*. In today's world of constant change there is still one constant, you're either selling or dying. Tune in on iTunes or your favorite podcast app – just search for *Sell or Die*.

AWARD FOR PRESENTATION EXCELLENCE. In 1997, Jeffrey was awarded the designation of Certified Speaking Professional (CSP) by the National Speakers Association. The CSP award has been given fewer than 500 times in the past 25 years and is the association's highest earned designation.

SPEAKER HALL OF FAME. In August 2008, Jeffrey was inducted into the National Speaker Association's Speaker Hall of Fame. The designation CPAE (Counsel of Peers Award for Excellence) honors professional speakers who have reached the top echelon of performance excellence. Each candidate must demonstrate mastery in seven categories: originality of material, uniqueness of style, experience, delivery, image, professionalism, and communication. To date, 191 of the world's greatest speakers have been inducted including Ronald Reagan, Art Linkletter, Colin Powell, Norman Vincent Peale, Earl Nightingale, and Zig Ziglar.

Jeffrey Gitomer's Philosophy of Sales and Life:

I give value first.
I help other people.
I strive to be the best at what I love to do.
I establish long-term relationships with everyone.

I have fun (and I do that every day).

"If you want to gain wealth, first gain a wealth of knowledge."

– Jeffrey Gitomer

BUYGITOMER

310 Arlington Avenue, Loft 329, Charlotte, North Carolina, 28203
www.gitomer.com 704/333-1112 helpme@gitomer.com

Notes

Notes

Notes

Notes

Notes

Notes